Korean Spirituality

DIMENSIONS OF ASIAN SPIRITUALITY

Shinto: The Way Home
Thomas P. Kabulis

Chan Buddhism
Peter D. Hershock

Korean Spirituality
Don Baker

Ancient Chinese Divination
Stephen L. Field

Korean Spirituality

DON BAKER

UNIVERSITY OF HAWAI'I PRESS

Honolulu

DIMENSIONS OF ASIAN SPIRITUALITY
Henry Rosemont, Jr., General Editor

*This series makes available short but comprehensive works on specific Asian
philosophical and religious schools of thought, works focused on a specific region, and
works devoted to the full articulations of a concept central to one or more of Asia's
spiritual traditions. Series volumes are written by distinguished scholars in the field who
not only present their subject matter in historical context for the nonspecialist reader,
but also express their own views of the contemporary spiritual relevance of their
subject matter for global citizens of the twenty-first century.*

Library of Congress Cataloging-in-Publication Data
Baker, Don (Donald L.)
Korean spirituality / Don Baker.
p. cm. — (Dimensions of Asian spirituality)
Includes bibliographical references and index.
ISBN 978-0-8248-3233-9 (hardcover: alk. paper) —
ISBN 978-0-8248-3257-5 (paperback: alk. paper)
1. Korea — Religion. 2. Spirituality — Korea. I. Title.
BL2230.B35 2008
200.9519 — dc22
2007035185

University of Hawai'i Press books are printed on acid-free
paper and meet the guidelines for permanence and
durability of the Council on Library Resources.

Designed by Rich Hendel

Printed by the Maple-Vail Book Manufacturing Group

Contents

Editor's Preface

ABOUT THIS SERIES

The University of Hawai'i Press has long been noted for its commitment to issuing high-quality scholarly publications in the field of Asian studies. The Press launched the Dimensions of Asian Spirituality series in keeping with that commitment. This is a most appropriate time for such a series. A number of the world's major and minor religions originated in Asia, and they continue to influence the lives of almost half of the world's population. Asian religions should now be seen as global in scope and impact, with rich and varied resources for the people of the twenty-first century.

Religion is at the heart of every culture. To be sure, the members of every culture have also been influenced by climate, geology, and the consequent patterns of economic activity they developed for the production and distribution of goods. Only a minimal knowledge of physical geography is necessary to understand why African sculptors largely employed wood as their medium, while their Italian Renaissance brethren usually worked with marble. Matters of geography and economics are necessary for understanding cultures—including our own—but they are not sufficient: wood and marble are also found in China, yet Chinese sculptors carved Confucian sages, Daoist immortals, and Buddhist bodhisattvas from those materials, not *chiwaras* or pietàs.

In the same way, a mosque, synagogue, cathedral, stupa, and pagoda may be equally beautiful, but they are beautiful in different ways, and the differences cannot be accounted for merely on the basis of the materials used in their construction. Their beauty, their ability to inspire awe and invite contemplation, rests largely on the religious view of the world—and the place of human beings in that world—that inspired and is expressed in their architecture. Thus the spiritual dimensions of a culture are reflected significantly not only in art and architecture, but also in music, myths, poetry, rituals, customs, and patterns of social behavior. It therefore follows that if we wish to understand why and how members of other cultures live as they do, we must understand the religious beliefs and practices to which they adhere.

In the first instance, such understanding of the "other" leads to tolerance, which is surely a good thing. Much of the pain and suffering in the world today is attributable to intolerance, a fear and hatred of those who look, think, and act differently. But as technological changes in communication, production, and transportation shrink the world, more and more people must confront the fact of human diversity both between and within nation-states. Hence there is a growing need to go beyond mere tolerance of difference to an appreciation and celebration of it.

The evils attendant upon intolerance are not to be minimized, but tolerance alone cannot contribute substantively to making the world a better and more sustainable place for human beings to live. Mere tolerance is easy because it is passive: I can fully respect your right to believe and worship as you wish, associate with whomever you wish, and say what you will, simply by ignoring you. Yet for most of us who live in economically developed societies or who are among the affluent in developing nations, tolerance is not enough. Ignoring the poverty, disease, and gross inequalities that afflict fully a third of the human race will exacerbate, not alleviate, the conditions responsible for the misery that generates the violence becoming ever more common throughout the world today.

Some would have us believe that religion is—as it supposedly always has been—the root cause of the world's violence and therefore should be done away with. This view is reinforced by invoking distorted accounts of the cosmologies of the world's religions, and pointing out that they are incompatible with much that we know of the world today from science.

But religions are not going to go away, nor should they. Those who see only the negative influences of religion—influences not to be ignored—are taking "a printed bill of fare as the equivalent for a solid meal," to quote William James. Worse than that, to point the finger at religion as responsible for most of the world's violence today is to obscure a far more important root cause: poverty. On this view, violence will cease only when the more fortunate among the peoples of the world become active, not passive, take up the plight of the less fortunate, and resolve to create and maintain a more just world, a resolve that requires a full appreciation of the co-humanity of everyone, significant differences in religious beliefs and practices notwithstanding.

Such appreciation should not, of course, oblige people to endorse all of the beliefs and practices followed by adherents of other religions, just as we may object to certain beliefs and practices within our own faiths. A growing number of Catholics, for instance, support a married clergy, the ordination of women, recognition of rights for gays and lesbians, and full reproductive rights for women. Yet they remain Catholics, believing that the tenets of their faith have the conceptual resources to justify and bring about these changes. In the same way, we can also believe, as a number of Muslim women do, that the *Quran* and other Islamic theological writings contain the conceptual resources to overcome the inferior status of women in some Muslim countries. Indeed, we can believe that every spiritual tradition has within it the resources to counter older practices inimical to the full flourishing of all the faithful—and of the faithful of other traditions, as well.

Another reason to go beyond mere tolerance to appreciation and celebration of the many and varied forms of spiritual expression is virtually a truism: the more we look through a window onto another culture's beliefs and practices, the more the window becomes a mirror of our own culture (even for those who follow no religious tradition). We must look very carefully and charitably, however, lest the reflections become distorted. When studying other religions, most people are strongly inclined to focus on cosmological and ontological questions: What do these people believe about how the world came to be, what it is, and where it is heading? Do they believe in ghosts? Immortal souls? A creator god?

Answering these and related metaphysical questions is of course necessary for fully understanding and appreciating the specific forms and content of the art, music, architecture, rituals, and traditions inspired by the specific religion under study. But the sensitive—and sensible—student will bracket the further question of whether the metaphysical pronouncements are literally true. We must attend carefully to the metaphysics and theologies of the religions we study, but questions of their literal truth should be set aside to concentrate on a different question: how could a thoughtful, thoroughly decent human being subscribe to and follow these beliefs and attendant practices? Studied in this light, we may come to see and appreciate how each religious tradition provides a coherent account of a world not fully amenable to human manipulation, nor perhaps even to full human understanding. The metaphysical pronouncements of the world's religions differ from faith to faith, exerting a significant influence on the physical expressions of each faith, their synagogues, stupas, mosques, pagodas, and cathedrals. Despite these differences among the buildings, however, the careful and sensitive observer can see the shared spiritual dimensions of human life that these sacred structures express, and in the same way we can come to see and appreciate the spiritual dimensions shared by each religion's unique metaphysics and theology. While the several religious traditions give different answers to the question of the meaning *of* life, they all provide a multiplicity of guidelines and spiritual disciplines to enable everyone to find meaning *in* life, in this world.

By plumbing the spiritual depths of other religious traditions, then, we may come to more deeply explore the spiritual resources of our own, at the same time diminishing the otherness of the "other" and creating a more peaceable and just world in which everyone can find meaning in their all-too-human lives.

ABOUT THIS VOLUME

Against this background we may turn more directly to the third offering in the Dimensions of Asian Spirituality series, *Korean Spirituality* by Don Baker. It is a most appropriate work to appear at this time for a number of reasons. Perhaps most importantly, the spirituality of Korea provides a model of how adherents of very different faith traditions can get on quite peaceably with their neighbors, interacting daily and closely rather than merely tolerating others at a distance. That the Koreans are a fairly homogeneous society is not to be denied, but there is more to the story than that. The perpetrators of sectarian violence in such areas as Iraq, Northern Ireland, and Kashmir, for example, claim different religious allegiances but are ethnically identical. How do the Koreans interpret their varied faiths so as to preserve harmony with their larger social, political, and cultural order?

A second reason for the timeliness of this volume is that it illustrates how different religions can inspire and modify one another when they are at peace with each other, a significant lesson to learn in the increasingly global community the world is becoming. Professor Baker uses as his central thread a tension between a sense of human frailty he ascribes to the Korean ethos and models of human perfectibility that originated in China but that the Koreans made altogether their own. Baker makes a good case for this dual orientation and illustrates clearly how it has affected Koreans' adoption and alteration of a number of spiritual traditions, from the continuing role of folk religion in contemporary society to the manifold Protestant and Buddhist sects, as well as the enduring influence of Confucianism as a way of life, the status of the Roman Catholic church, and the uniquely Korean interpretations of Buddhism (e.g., Won) and Christianity (e.g., the reverend Sun Myung Moon).

Still another reason why *Korean Spirituality* is an important book today is that Baker devotes a closing section of the volume to North Korean expressions of religiosity through the concept of *juche* (self-sufficiency), which he well demonstrates has spiritual dimensions no less than political and moral ones.

All of these are important reasons for reading this book, but there is another: the intrinsic interest of seeing how others confront a world not of their own making, which can only help us better understand how we confront that world, too.

HENRY ROSEMONT, JR.

Acknowledgments

When I was first approached about contributing a volume on Korean spirituality to the Dimensions of Asian Spirituality series, my first reaction was to decline. I wasn't sure if I could deal adequately with the complexity and diversity of Korean spirituality in one slender volume. However, the series editor encouraged me to search for common themes across the wide spectrum of religious and spiritual beliefs and practices in Korean culture, past and present. Once I began producing chapters under his guidance, he wielded an editorial scalpel that excised much of my verbose prose and raised questions that stimulated me to look at old material in new ways and see connections I hadn't noticed before. The result is the book you now hold in your hand, a distillation of an academic career spent observing and analyzing Korean spirituality.

I first went to Korea in 1971. The U.S. Peace Corps sent me to Kwangju, a provincial capital in the southwest corner of the peninsula, to teach English to seventh and eighth graders. It was an eye-opening experience. Korea was then a poor country ruled by a dictator, former general Park Chung Hee, but the rich diversity of Korean culture was still evident. I spent many hours wandering the urban streets and rural paths of Korea and discovering what a wide-ranging spiritual tradition Korea had. On city streets I saw crosses marking Christian churches and heard the drums of shamanic rituals. In the countryside I saw Buddhist monks chanting in mountain temples and elderly men conversing within the walls of Confucian academies. The beauty and complexity of Korean culture that I observed in the Kwangju region made me determined to learn more about Korea after I returned to North America.

After three years in Kwangju, I moved back across the Pacific Ocean to attend the University of Washington, where I was fortunate enough to work on a doctorate in Korean history under James Palais. Jim passed away in 2006, but even now his influence lingers. Often when I am about to embark on a research project, I ask myself,

"What sorts of questions would Jim ask of this material?" I wish Jim were alive today so he could read this book and tell me whether I've been faithful to his example of wringing out of the data all the information and insights it can provide, without making conclusions the data won't support.

After finishing at the University of Washington, I ended up a couple of hundred kilometers up the road, in the Department of Asian Studies at the University of British Columbia in Vancouver. There I've been fortunate to have such colleagues as Dan Overmyer, Jinhua Chen, and Nam-lin Hur, who have taught me about religion and spirituality elsewhere in East Asia.

Vancouver has been my home for the last twenty years, providing an invigorating atmosphere for exploring Korean spirituality. Vancouver is a Pacific Rim city, so I don't have to travel far to observe Asian spirituality. Within a short drive from my home I can find a Japanese Pure Land temple, a Chinese Chan temple, a Hindu Vedanta center, a Sikh gurdwara, and a South Asian mosque. The Korean Catholic church is about a twenty-minute drive away, and five minutes beyond it stands a Korean Buddhist temple. There are also close to two hundred Korean Protestant churches scattered across the greater Vancouver region. Sometimes I feel that I don't even need to travel to Korea to study Korean spirituality.

One of the other benefits of living in a Pacific Rim city like Vancouver is that Korean scholars come here for research during their sabbatical leaves. I have benefited from meeting Ahn Youngsang, Bang In, Chang Sukman, Choi Jong Seong, Kang In-cheol, Kim Eunjong, and Ryu Jong Son, all of whom shared their insights into Korean religion and spirituality with me. Also, Ken Kangnam Oh, recently retired from teaching Asian religion at the University of Regina, has met with me many times to discuss the state of Korean spirituality today.

Even though I learned much in Vancouver, I still traveled to Korea frequently to observe Korean spirituality in Korea itself. (Both the Korea Foundation and the Fulbright Korean-American Educational Commission have funded such research trips of mine over the years.) So many people helped me in Korea that it is impossible to name them all. However, there were some who went so far out of their way to help me with my research that I would be derelict if I didn't mention their names. When I was still a graduate student, Choi Suk-woo, the director of the Center for the Study of Korean Church History, helped me immensely by providing documents I needed to look at. Fr. Choi also introduced me to Keum Jang-t'ae when we were both graduate students. In the years since, Keum's many books have cleared a lot of brambles from the path to a better understanding of Korean Confucianism. The late Shim Jaeryong did the same for Korean Buddhism in conversation and with his publications.

Others who provided special assistance in Korea include two Americans: Frank Tedesco, who was active in Korean Buddhist circles, and Dave Mason, who has trekked all over Korea taking photographs of shrines to mountain gods. I was also helped by Park Chung-shin, a professor of Christian Studies at Soongsil University in Seoul. Australian scholar Paul Beirne helped me understand the early years of Tonghak, and Youn Jae-keun did the same with regard to Daesun Jinri-hoe. For aid in understanding Won Buddhism, I am indebted to Park Kwang-soo.

Anyone who is familiar with the English-language scholarship on Korean religion will recognize the influence of Robert E. Buswell, Jr., on what I write about Korean Buddhism, Laurel Kendall and Boudewijn Walraven on what I write about shamanism, Michael Kalton on what I write about Confucianism, and Don Clark and James Grayson on what I write about Christianity. I have learned much from them, both in conversation and from reading their writings.

Closer to home, I should acknowledge the support of family. My parents, Don and Carrie Baker, are still both active and healthy at the age of ninety-two, so they've had many decades to wonder at their Louisiana-raised son's obsession with things Korean. Though they probably would have preferred that I go into law, as so many of my relatives did, they never complained about my departure from family tradition into the halls of academia. In fact, they've encouraged my scholarly ambitions and have even accepted my leaving our native country to teach at a university in Canada.

I owe a special debt of thanks to my wife, Yumi, who wasn't particularly interested in exploring her homeland's religious traditions until I started asking her to accompany me on field trips to sacred

mountains and urban worship halls. She has been such an understanding and supportive traveling companion that I've started introducing her in Korea as both my wife and my research assistant.

And, of course, I also have to express my gratitude to Patricia
Crosby of the University of Hawai'i Press, without whose strong support the Dimensions of Asian Spirituality series (of which this volume
is a part) would never have materialized. It was Pat who convinced
me that this book needed to be written and that I could write it. She
is a legend in our field for her efforts to ensure that a wide range of
English-language scholarship on Asia finds its way into print.

Despite all that I have learned from so many people over so many
years, readers of this text may nevertheless discover errors of fact
or interpretation in it. I accept full responsibility for any mistakes.
I hope such flaws as there may be will encourage readers to seek out
additional sources of information on Korean spirituality. The suggested readings at the back of this volume can serve as a start, but
there is more material available than could be listed in that brief bib-
liography. Go to a library, go online, or go to Korea. Go wherever
your thirst for knowledge leads you, and enjoy exploring the fasci-
nating landscape that is Korean spirituality.

CHAPTER 1

Korean Spirituality
A Multiplicity of Approaches to Transcending the Human Condition

A few years ago, I kept a small apartment in one of the most modern districts of one of the most modern cities on the Korean peninsula. Within a short walk from that apartment in the Songp'a district of Seoul, the capital of the Republic of Korea (South Korea), I could reach both a huge shopping mall with hundreds of crowded shops and a bustling Buddhist temple drawing large crowds of worshippers. There were medical clinics around the corner and a shaman's office up the street. At the intersection nearest to that apartment, a Christian bookstore selling books on how to get to heaven shared a corner with a Daoist center teaching physical exercises and breathing techniques that promised health and longevity. If I walked a couple of blocks in any direction, I would see enough churches, temples, and other architectural signs of religious activity to convince me that Koreans were a highly spiritual people.

The spirituality seen in Seoul and throughout the Korean peninsula is the focus of this book. Korea provides a particularly fruitful laboratory for the study of spirituality in the modern world because of the great variety of religious, philosophical, and spiritual beliefs and practices found there. Korea offers its people a wider range of spiritual and religious techniques for addressing the problems of life than do countries such as Italy or Pakistan that have a single dominant religion. Koreans can choose from polytheist, monotheist, or nontheist conceptions of invisible powers greater than themselves. They can seek solutions to the difficulties they encounter through prayer, meditation, study, chanting, somber ritual, or playful interaction with gods and spirits. They can choose from several different sacred calendars to determine which times are best for approaching the invisible forces that they believe wield influence over their lives. And they can choose from different sacred geographies when deciding which places are best for making such approaches. Though Korea is ethnically homogeneous, in its widely varied spirituality it resembles multicultural societies such as the United States and Canada, with the significant difference that in Korea there is no single dominant religion and thus less peer pressure to conform to a dominant mode of spirituality.

Korea in the twenty-first century is quite different from the Korea of only a few decades ago, but its spiritual problematic has remained fairly constant for two thousand years. Koreans tend to assume that human beings are essentially good. They also recognize that human beings often act in inappropriate ways. The long history of Korean spirituality is a history of attempts to resolve this contradiction. Generally speaking, people who see themselves as a mixture of good and evil can more easily accept failure, because they don't expect perfection. Most Koreans, on the other hand, have not had the excuse of inborn human weakness to fall back on. Koreans assume that they are endowed with innate virtue, which has made it difficult for them to explain their continuing failure to achieve the perfection they have expected to be theirs by birthright. Frustrated by their inability to solve this dilemma, they have moved from folk religion through Buddhism and Neo-Confucianism to Christianity and newer religions in a millennia-long search for an explanation of human moral frailty and a way to overcome it.

Koreans now address that problematic in an environment radically different from the environment their ancestors lived in only a short while ago. In the second half of the twentieth century, following liberation from Japanese colonial rule (1910–1945) and the fraternal fighting and devastation of the Korean War (1950–1953), South Koreans undertook a march to modernity that transformed the non-Communist southern half of the peninsula from a poor, rural society into one that is both urban and wealthy. Per capita annual income in South Korea was only $82 in 1961; a few years into the twenty-first century, it surpassed $15,000. At the same time, so many Koreans moved to Seoul and other cities that by the end of the century almost four out of every five South Koreans lived in cities, though in 1960 three out of four Koreans lived in villages and small towns.

While they were growing richer and more urban, Koreans also transformed their nation's landscape. Where only a few decades ago there were dirt paths, rice paddies, and thatched-roof homes, now there are broad thoroughfares, shopping malls, rapid-transit lines, and high-rise condominium and office towers. Moreover, scattered among the high-rises are thousands of churches and temples that were not there before, catering to an increasingly religious population.

The Korean government counted only 10,366 buildings used for religious rituals in 1962, excluding shaman shrines. They found 58,896 such buildings in 1993, an increase of more than 500 percent. Though different religious communities added new worship halls at different rates, at the end of the twentieth century all of Korea's major religious organizations (with the exception of Confucianism) provided substantially more places for their followers to gather than they ever had before in Korean history. For example, the number of Buddhist temples in South Korea rose from 2,306 in 1962 to 11,561 in 1997, a five-fold increase over a little more than three decades. The numbers are even more remarkable for Protestant churches. There were at least 58,046 Protestant churches in South Korea in 1997, more than eight times as many as the 6,785 reported in 1962. Catholics are not able to establish new churches as quickly, primarily because of a shortage of priests. Nevertheless, there were 1,366 Catholic parish churches in Korea in 2005, compared to only 313 in 1965, a respectable fourfold increase over forty years. Even the relatively small indigenous religion of Won Buddhism (which, despite its name, considers itself a new religion rather than a branch of Korean Buddhism) expanded from 131 worship halls in 1969 to 418 in 1997, indicating that the boom in organized religion has not been confined to religious organizations with a long history and international connections.

Despite the architectural evidence of growing religious fervor in South Korea, only slightly more than half of the South Korean population professes a specific religious orientation. However, that too is a substantial change from the past. The first time anyone tried to count the number of religious Koreans was soon after Korea fell under Japanese colonial rule. In 1916, Japanese authorities counted approximately five hundred and thirty thousand Koreans who were enrolled in various Christian, Buddhist, sectarian Shinto, or Korean indigenous new religious organizations, out of a population of between fifteen and seventeen million. That was only around 3 percent of the Korean population at that time. As recently as 1964, the government of Korea calculated that only 3.5 million out of its 28.2 million citizens had a specific religious affiliation. However, the number of Koreans calling themselves Buddhists or Christians grew rapidly from the late 1960s through the late 1990s. By the end of the twentieth century, government figures as well as Gallup surveys indicated that more than one out of every two Koreans had come to consider themselves religious.

A government census in 2005 confirmed this dramatic shift toward identification with specific religious communities. In that census, 53 percent of Koreans said they had a religious affiliation, while only 47 percent said they were not Buddhists, Christians, or members of any other religious community. According to that census, 10.7 million Koreans (23%) were Buddhists, 8.6 million (18%) were Protestant Christians, and 5.3 million (11%) were Catholics. An additional half a million were members of smaller religious communities, such as Confucianism or one of Korea's many new religions, such as Won Buddhism. (Participants in Korea's folk religion, shamanism, do not appear in those census figures because neither the government nor the average Korean considers shamanism a religion. Instead, shamanism is viewed as a part of Korean cultural tradition.)

Those census figures almost surely underestimate the number of Koreans who engage in religious activity. Anyone who has spent much time in South Korea in recent decades probably has noticed the large numbers of people who hike up mountain trails on fall weekends to pray at Buddhist temples, though many of those pilgrims, if they are asked about their religious beliefs, will insist they are not Buddhists and have no religious affiliation. Similarly, many of the clients who patronize the shamans who can be found in every city and town in Korea will, if questioned, state that they do not believe in shamanism. There are also many new religions in Korea that would not survive if survey results revealing their numbers were accurate. For example, in its 2005 census, the government found very few who gave their religious affiliation as Daesun Jinri-hoe, though that new religion receives enough contributions from believers every year to operate a university and several high schools as well as a major hospital complex and a large charitable foundation.

Clearly, there are many people in Korea who hold beliefs we normally associate with religion or engage in activities that appear religious even though they say they are not religious. To understand how this can be, it is helpful to distinguish between religiosity and spirituality. "Spiritual" and "religious" are sometimes treated as synonymous terms, but I believe we will better understand Korean spirituality and religion if we differentiate the terms.

Spirituality can be defined as attitudes and actions grounded in the belief that there are invisible forces more powerful than we are, and that through interaction with those forces we can better ourselves or make our lives more pleasant or meaningful. Religiosity, in contrast, has a more restricted reference than spirituality. To me, religiosity refers to spirituality expressed within a specific institutional framework and motivated by a more clearly defined sense of the nature of those invisible forces. Thus, all those who are religious are also spiritual, but not everyone who is spiritual is also religious. For instance, it has recently become common for some North Americans to describe themselves as "spiritual but not religious." By that, they usually mean that they are not members of any organized religion and that they believe in some supernatural force or presence but do not feel the need for a detailed definition of who or what that supernatural force is. Spirituality that is not religiosity is more diffuse and individual than religiosity. Someone who is spiritual but not religious does not normally attend a house of worship regularly and does not subscribe to a specific set of religious doctrines; instead, such a person feels he or she can believe in and interact with invisible forces in whatever way he or she feels most appropriate. In Korea, both spirituality and religion entail interaction with invisible forces for the purposes of self-cultivation or the improvement of the conditions under which we live, but spirituality is broader than religiosity in that it can take place either within or outside a religious organization. Religiosity, on the other hand, implies joining together with like-minded individuals in a social organization defined by a common understanding of what sorts of invisible forces members should interact with, how and when they should do so, and what roles various members should play in that interaction. For example, a Korean who patronizes shamans may do so when plagued by health or financial problems that she has not been able to resolve through more mundane means; she may therefore feel in need of supernatural assistance. This troubled Korean might also approach the spirits directly without the intercession of a shaman, or she might ask a Buddhist monk to perform an appropriate ritual.

We would not be justified in calling such a person a Buddhist or a "shamanist." Someone should not be labeled religious, or a believer in a specific religion, unless she gives priority to one particular approach to the supernatural and agrees to let an organization that embodies that approach tell her what she can and cannot believe and do if she wants to maintain good relations with those spirits. Such a person could, however, be called spiritual, because she recognizes the existence of spiritual entities and believes that human beings should take the existence of those entities into account when attempting to overcome problems encountered in everyday life.

In premodern Korea, the only people we would label religious are religious "professionals" such as Buddhist monks. However, if we look at the earliest written accounts of life on the Korean peninsula, from almost two thousand years ago, it is clear that from the beginning of their history, Koreans have believed in spirits and have tried to negotiate with those spirits for better living conditions. It is also clear that some Koreans came to believe that if they wanted to have better living conditions, they had to become better people, because they believed that they themselves were ultimately responsible for anything unpleasant or unfortunate that happened to them. "Spirituality" is the term we can give to this search for better relations with the spiritual realm and this desire for moral self-improvement. It was only over the last couple of centuries, and particularly over the past fifty years, that large numbers of Koreans came to believe that negotiations with spiritual beings or the cultivation of a better moral character were best done within a clearly defined institutional structure. This rise in religiosity reveals itself in the growing percentage of the Korean population claiming a particular religious affiliation.

Religiosity, although popular, is relatively new to Koreans; but they have been a highly spiritual people for millennia. A defining characteristic of spirituality is a search for transcendence, in the sense of transcending the limitations of normal human existence and normal human capabilities. Conceptions of what needs to be transcended differ, however. Many spiritual and religious traditions emphasize transcending the limitations of the body and the material realm in which it is immersed. Koreans traditionally have preferred to focus instead on transcending the limitations of individuality, without giving much thought to differences between the material (the body) and the immaterial (the soul). In either case, transcendence is pursued as a solution to the problems inherent in the human condition. Those problems are the same the world over: poverty, illness, pain, suffering, and death are visible in every human community. Human beings, no matter where they live, may also suffer as a result of acts of nature such as hurricanes, earthquakes, or floods. Moreover, evil behavior is another human problem that seems to be universal.

Spiritual beliefs and religious teachings offer explanations for why human beings encounter the problems they encounter, along with suggestions for how to overcome them. Spiritual and religious assumptions about the fundamental nature of reality, for example, provide peace of mind by giving us conceptual tools for understanding what would otherwise be an unintelligible world. Such teachings offer us hope that, by utilizing certain techniques, we can influence what happens to us and exercise some measure of control over our lives. Without that hope, many people would live their lives in abject terror, never knowing what was going to happen next and feeling helpless in the face of whatever cards fate dealt them.

A typical unexplainable and unpreventable human event is death. Human beings want to know why we and our loved ones have to die. Moreover, we usually would like to postpone those deaths for as long as possible. A typical religious account of death states that this material world is but our temporary home, and death releases us to move on to our true home, often envisioned as paradise. However, religions also often promise that sincere requests to powerful supernatural beings may gain us some extra time in this temporary home or may make our stay here less miserable while we wait to move on.

Another issue religions must wrestle with is the origin of evil. Some religious traditions blame evil spirits, such as Satan, for evil in this world. Others insist that we bear the blame ourselves, because we let our minds or our bodies lead us astray. Different assumptions about the roots of evil lead to different assumptions about how best to combat it. If we believe that evil spirits are responsible for something unfortunate that befalls us, then it is likely that we will try to ally with one or more powerful gods to fight against those evil spirits. However, if we believe that our bodies are the greatest source of danger, we are more likely to emphasize disciplining the body with ascetic practices as the best defense against evil. Koreans have traditionally blamed our existence as separate, distinct individuals for most of the difficulties human beings encounter. They have therefore tended to seek solutions to ubiquitous human problems by transcending individuality through identification with a larger community. This group orientation reveals itself both in the way Koreans traditionally have tried to explain death and in the way they have tried to explain evil. For example, rather than offering hope that a person can look forward to a better and longer life in the world after this one, traditional Korean religions have tended to talk less about personal immortality and more about the eternal, or at least long-term, survival of the group to which the individual belongs. Immortality comes from being remembered by your descendants or students and being honored by them with ritual. Their memory of you keeps your ties with that community alive long after you are gone and provides a shared experience that can help define that community and keep it together. This vision of immortality leads Koreans to honor the departed with regular group commemorative rituals long after their death.

Evil is also explained within this framework that ascribes higher value to the group than to the individual. Koreans have traditionally assumed that human beings are born virtuous; there was no doctrine of original sin in pre-Christian Korean traditions. However, Koreans have long been aware that human beings do not always act properly. The traditional explanation is that human beings think of themselves as individuals, which causes them to act at odds with the communities of which they are members. It is that pursuit of individual interest at the expense of the larger community that introduces evil into this world. Therefore, forming a personal alliance with a powerful spirit or punishing our bodies are not good ways to fight evil. Instead, we should remind ourselves that we don't exist in isolation from the people and things around us. If we forge closer ties with the other members of our community, we will transcend our individuality and therefore move farther away from our preoccupation with personal benefit, a preoccupation that is the root of all evil. To encourage us to think and act communally, Korean spiritual leaders tend to promote an ethics of harmonious interpersonal interaction. They point out that all human beings are members of families, residents of neighborhoods, and classmates or workmates of other human beings, and that they should act as such.

A worldwide survey of religions and spirituality suggests that religions that place the highest value on the individual, such as Christianity and Islam, tend to place more emphasis on theology than on ethics. That is because God is the fountainhead of ethical obligations in such religions, and the relationship between the individual and God is therefore more important than the relationship between any one human individual and another. Such religions also tend to focus on the personal consequences of fidelity to, or violation of, God's commands. That is why heaven and hell are so important in those two religions. Heaven and hell exist to reward or punish individuals posthumously for what they did while they were alive.

Moreover, such individualistic religions tend to portray the spiritual struggle to promote good and resist evil as a battle between the material world we live in and the immaterial realm of God and the rewards He promises the righteous after death. A spirituality that values individuality often gives that individuality an immaterial foundation (e.g., an individual soul). Belief in an immaterial individual soul allows those within such traditions to blame material existence for keeping them where they are now, confined to the realm of matter, and keeping them from where they are meant to be, in paradise with God.

The traditional religions of Korea, on the other hand, tend to place more emphasis on ethics than on theology. Because their primary concern is the group rather than the individual, the moral codes that govern interaction within the group are given priority. Any individual's particular relationship with a supernatural being is important primarily for the impact it has on the cohesiveness of the group. Therefore, traditional Korean forms of spirituality place less emphasis on personal rewards after death than on the impact an individual's behavior can have on that individual's family, village, or society. In addition, both the individual and the community of which he or she is a part are composed of matter, which means there is less interest in overcoming the limitations of the material world and more interest in connections within that material world. Such connections are valuable because they provide a way to overcome the limitations of isolated individuality.

However, one cannot draw a hard-and-fast line between a non-Korean spirituality that focuses on transcending the material world and a traditional Korean spirituality that focuses instead on transcending individuality. There are many examples of Koreans striving to transcend the limitations of material existence, even before Christian books and missionaries introduced the distinction between a material body and an immaterial soul and insisted on the primary importance of a personal relationship between an individual and God. Korea, like China, had a tradition of mountain hermits who fled their villages and families in pursuit of immortality. Korea also has ascetic strands in its history of Buddhism; even today, some Buddhist monks show their lack of attachment to their bodies by burning their fingers. Similarly, Christianity and Islam have also had adherents, most notably their mystics, who focused on transcending the limitations of individuality. The Korean focus on overcoming the limitations of individual existence and the Christian-Islamic focus on overcoming the limitations of material existence are best described as differences in emphasis, rather than as the total exclusion of one orientation or the other.

Despite these differences, spirituality in Korea is essentially one manifestation of the universal human desire to transcend the limitations of individual human existence and overcome suffering. In Korea and around the world, the spiritual pursuit of those goals is usually distinguished from other ways of pursuing them by a reliance on the cooperation of supernatural beings.

Spirituality operates within a worldview constructed from various ethical, cosmological, and ontological premises asserting that we can predict the otherwise unpredictable, explain the otherwise unexplainable, and control the otherwise uncontrollable by interacting with, receiving communications from, and even influencing the behavior of powerful invisible beings or forces. In the religious version of spirituality, such invisible forces are supernatural personalities who are introduced to humanity through myths and revelation and are approached through ritual and prayer.

We shouldn't confuse religiosity and spirituality with science, which also deals with invisible forces. Korea has long had "science," but many of its sciences were quite different from what is meant by that term in the modern world. It is often difficult to distinguish between spirituality and premodern science in Korea. For example, there were astronomers in premodern Korea, but they also functioned as astrologers, drawing implications for human behavior on the earth below from their observations of the skies above. There were also geographers in premodern Korea, but they were experts in feng shui as well. They were supposed to identify the invisible rivers of energy that flowed through the ground and suggest ways to utilize that energy. Medical doctors existed in premodern Korea, but many medical books combined chants and prayers with acupuncture and herbal prescriptions as a way to improve the invisible flow of energy through the body.

A blurring of the boundaries occurred between premodern science and religion in Korea because both were concerned with interactions between human beings and invisible forces. We can make an analytical distinction between the two today because what we now label science focuses on that part of the universe, both visible and invisible, that is devoid of the quirks of personality. However, because both religion and science seek to minimize the uncertainties of life and give human beings a greater sense of control over their environment and their fate, in traditional societies religion and science were usually collaborators rather than rivals. Traditional Korea was one such society. Religions in Korea promoted certain approaches to medicine, geography, and astronomy, and their distinctive conceptions of the human body, the earth, and the celestial realm demonstrate how a spiritual worldview can influence attitudes toward the natural world.

Placing supernatural beings within the larger category of "invisible forces" in our working definition of spirituality also allows us to discuss two philosophies that sometimes are called "religious," even though they lack a conception of God. We call Buddhist philosophy (unlike popular Buddhist religion) and Confucianism "nontheistic" rather than "atheistic" because the term "atheism" implies the active rejection of the concept of God. Rather, Buddhist philosophers and neo-Confucians are nontheists, people for whom the notion of God's existence is irrelevant or for whom the question of whether or not God exists never arises.

Religious conviction implies belief in a supernatural being or beings; thus, Buddhist philosophy and Neo-Confucianism are not religious in the usual meaning of the term. However, they represent forms of spirituality because they both assume that there are invisible forces much more powerful than any individual human being. In Buddhism one invisible force is karma, the law of moral causation decreeing that the invisible fruits of our thoughts and actions in this life will determine what happens to us in the next. In Neo-Confucianism, *li* is an important invisible force. *Li* is the cosmic network of appropriate interactions that determines how human beings and everything else in the universe should behave. Both Buddhism and Neo-Confucianism assume that if we act the way such invisible forces encourage us to act, we can become better human beings and also create a much healthier, safer, and more predictable environment in which to live. No discussion of Korean spirituality can ignore the important roles Buddhist philosophy and Neo-Confucianism have played in Korean culture over the centuries, any more than it could ignore the concepts of the heavens, the earth, and the human body that religions borrowed from premodern science. In the chapters ahead, we will explore all these dimensions of Korean spirituality, from the religious to the nonreligious.

It is a journey well worth taking because of the unusual degree of diversity and complexity in Korean spirituality. There are many countries in the world with a substantial Christian population. There are also many with a substantial Buddhist population. However, South Korea may be the only country with a largely ethnically homogeneous population in which the numbers of Buddhists and Christians come so close to being evenly balanced. Furthermore, as we will see in chapter 2, South Korea may be the only industrialized nation in which folk religion remains vibrant and free of institutional trappings. Though Shinto in Japan and Hinduism in South Asia and Bali resemble folk religions in many ways, they are both much more institutionalized, with their canonized sacred texts and their ancient halls of worship, than Korea's folk religion.

Another unique feature of Korean spirituality is the great difference between North Korea and South Korea today. Though the entire Korean peninsula shared one religious culture before the split between a Communist north and a non-Communist south in 1945, they now are radically different. Most formal religious activity (with exceptions that will be discussed in an appendix) has been suppressed in North Korea. In South Korea, on the other hand, religious freedom has led to more religious activity and religious diversity than has ever before existed on the Korean peninsula. (In the pages that follow, "Korea" stands for South Korea, unless otherwise specified; South Korea is where the many forms of Korean spirituality can be most easily identified and examined.)

Because of the wide range of its ethical assumptions, theological beliefs, and spiritual practices, Korea provides a fertile landscape for exploring the many different forms spirituality can take. Let us now embark on that journey by exploring the various strands in the complex fabric that is Korean spirituality.

In order to render Korean spirituality more comprehensible, we need to extract the various threads of Korean spirituality from the fabric into which they are woven. Yet, if we treat those threads as though they represent separate and distinct religious and philosophical traditions, we oversimplify. Moreover, when we try to unravel those threads, we risk destroying the fabric they weave. Classification and analysis are made more difficult by the fact that Korean spirituality often manifests in the spaces between the lines delineating particular religious orientations. In addition, the threads in Korea's religious fabric are interwoven so tightly that it is often difficult to identify a particular manifestation of spirituality with a specific religious tradition.

The most efficient and least misleading way to analyze Korean spirituality and classify it into its component elements is to focus on the few religious and spiritual professionals rather than on the many casual lay practitioners. In traditional Korea, religious labels were used primarily for descriptions of religious specialists and their specific spiritual and religious traditions. Moreover, many of those descriptions came from the religious professionals themselves, who often find it in their own best interest to draw clear distinctions between their traditions and those of others. In a competitive religious environment, professionals need to convince the average man or woman that they offer an approach to solving problems that is both different from and better than what other specialists can offer. They affix brand names in the hope that proclaiming clear religious boundaries will help them win customer loyalty. However, we need to remind ourselves that the sectarian divisions proclaimed by religious professionals have less influence on the behavior and beliefs of the general public than the professionals would have us believe. If we remember that categories such as shamanism, Buddhism, Confucianism, and Daoism do not correspond precisely to the average Korean's perception of the spiritual and religious options open to him, then we can better understand how spirituality actually manifests in daily life.

Despite the variety of paths Koreans can choose from as they search for solutions to the problems of this world, we can identify some common elements in Korean spirituality. For example, Koreans—both laypeople and religious professionals—have traditionally sought to become sages. They have disagreed on the particulars of what defines a sage and how sagehood is best achieved, but they have all agreed that a sage is someone with exceptional wisdom. Wisdom in a sage means superior insight into both what should be done and how it should it done. A sage is someone who knows how to minimize and overcome the problems human beings inevitably encounter as they move from birth to death. In other words, a sage possesses usable knowledge. Koreans have been less interested in knowledge for knowledge's sake than in practical knowledge that can guide them past the shoals of life.

Because Koreans have been more interested in applying knowledge than in contemplating and savoring it, they have linked knowledge and action so closely that each is seen as incomplete without the other. A sage is not only someone who knows how to act appropriately; a sage is also someone who acts in accordance with that knowledge. You can't be considered a sage unless you act like one. What does it mean to act like a sage? A sage is someone whose actions promote the good of the whole over the good of a part of that whole. This could mean acting in the best interests of an extended family instead of in the particular interest of a member of that family at the expense of the whole family. It could mean acting in such a way that a whole village benefits from your actions and not just a particular family within that village. Or it could mean acting so that the entire national community—or even all humanity—benefits, rather than working to ensure that the primary beneficiary of your actions is yourself or your relatives, friends, or neighbors. In short, a sage is someone who acts out of concern for the common good rather than in pursuit of personal benefit. A sage is able to act this way, according to the traditional Korean view, because a sage sees the world with an impartial perspective. A sage is someone who can see what is best for everyone and then acts accordingly. Unbiased insight and motivation that is not self-centered inspires sages to act so that they promote harmony throughout the universe. Ideally, a sage would act in harmony with all the various components of the cosmos, from the family and the village community to everything found in heaven and on earth, such as stars and animals. This vision of sagehood has been articulated with different degrees of explicitness in Korea. From the very beginning of its recorded history, tension existed in Korea between the priority spiritual leaders placed on concern for the greater good and the concern individuals showed for solutions to their personal problems. Some religions accorded more legitimacy to self-interest than others. Even within different religious traditions, religious rituals for personal gain (such as health or wealth) coexisted with techniques for cultivating a less self-centered character. The uneasy coexistence of exhortations to disinterested pursuit of the common good alongside expressions of individual concern for self-interest continues today. A little more than two centuries ago, Christianity introduced to Koreans the notion of a saint. A saint differs from a sage in that devotion to God and obedience to his will are the identifying characteristics of a saint, as opposed to wisdom. Moreover, saints reap personal benefits after death from their obedience and devotion to God in this life. This exposure to the notion of sainthood and its emphasis on the individual's personal relationship with God made it easier for Koreans to imagine a form of spirituality that prioritizes the individual over the group. Nevertheless, despite the strength of Christianity today, the search for sagehood rather than sainthood remains the dominant theme in Korean spirituality.

Such emphasis on sagehood is a prescription for frustration. Who among us can be perfectly wise and act with a complete lack of self-interest on a regular basis? The likelihood of frustration is heightened by the deep-rooted assumption in Korea that human beings are born good. When Koreans say we are essentially good, they don't mean that we are morally perfect from birth. What they mean is that we are all born with virtuous instincts and, if we live in accordance with those instincts, we will live moral, selfless lives. Moreover, because we are virtuous by nature, we don't need help from any supernatural source to reach perfection. By merely fostering our own innate goodness, we should be able to become perfect through our own efforts.

However, Koreans have been realistic enough to recognize that there are very few, if any, perfect human beings. Why do so many of us fall short of perfection when we are innately virtuous? First of all, we find it difficult to gain clear and certain knowledge of how we should act. How can we act properly if we don't know the proper way to act? How can we work toward the greater good if we don't know what that greater good is or how to achieve it? Second, even on those rare occasions when we know exactly what we should do, we often fail to act as we should. Whenever we are forced to acknowledge a gap between what we know we should do and what we actually do, we become frustrated with our own moral frailty. A third cause of frustration stems from the fact that we are not alone in the universe. Even if we succeed in acting properly, if others in our environment—such as family members, neighbors, or even natural forces—fail to harmo-

as family members, neighbors, or even natural forces—fail to harmonize their actions with ours, then our attempts to promote harmony will be frustrated.

as family members, neighbors, or even natural forces—fail to harmonize their actions with ours, then our attempts to promote harmony will be frustrated. Furthermore, sagehood as Koreans define it remains tantalizingly just out of reach, even for the least self-centered among us, because the sage seeks to transcend individuality while remaining an individual in a world of other individuals. In other words, sagehood is an impossible dream; yet it is a dream Koreans never stopped dreaming and have seldom recognized as impossible.

For two millennia, Koreans have sought explanations for this gap between their assumption of human perfectibility and the reality of human moral frailty, explanations they hoped would provide techniques for bridging that gap. It is this search that has led them from folk religion to Buddhism and Neo-Confucianism and then in recent centuries to Christianity and new religions.

To understand why perfection was so difficult to achieve, Koreans needed a definition of imperfection and an explanation of what caused it. The traditional concept of imperfection identifies it with disharmony, whether within the human community or within the natural world. This is the Korean equivalent of what other traditions call "evil." In the Korean worldview, evil is not an abstract concept that can stand alone or that can be defined without reference to the particular situation in which it is created. Rather, evil appears when we do what we should not have done or when we do not do what we should have done. In other words, evil is a failure to act appropriately that introduces disharmony into our lives, our society, and our universe.

Unfortunately, despite the best of intentions, human beings cannot always act appropriately. The frustration Koreans felt at this inability to eliminate disharmony and evil was exacerbated by the difficulties they encountered in their pursuit of an explanation for the persistence of imperfection. They did not give up, however. Over the centuries, they have explored, and continue to explore, various highways and byways of religious and philosophical thought and practice in a quest for sagehood.

CHAPTER 2

Folk Religion and Animism

The Korean quest for sagehood had what would appear to be a most unlikely source: the loosely connected assortment of beliefs and practices we now call "folk religion." The term "sage" is not used in Korea's folk religion to refer to even the most advanced practitioners. (When that term does appear, it is a title for some of the deities those practitioners address in their rituals.) Nor is there much explicit talk of overcoming selfishness in order to act harmoniously with the cosmos. Those who seek the aid of the spirits in the folk pantheon are usually seeking to improve conditions for a larger community, such as their family or village. To the extent that practitioners of folk religion are concerned about what is best for others more than about what is best for themselves, they can be said to represent the Korean tradition of a spirituality directed toward the common good, even though they would not identify themselves as sages.

Nor, in traditional times, would they have identified themselves as practitioners of folk religion. The term "folk religion" wasn't applied to the traditional spirituality of the general population in Korea until the late nineteenth century. One problem with using that term is that the boundaries delineating folk religion are so faint that it is often difficult to distinguish where folk religion ends and other traditions begin. Shamans, the most visible practitioners of folk religion in Korea today, will tell you they are Buddhists if you ask their religion. That is partially because many of the gods who appear in their rituals are borrowed from Buddhism. But they also worship gods borrowed from Daoism, as well as many gods and spirits neither Buddhist nor Daoist. In addition, their rituals have little in common with the rituals seen in the main halls of Buddhist temples. Another blurring of boundaries is seen in traditional community rituals, both those promoted by the state and those centered on villages, which often add Confucian elements to a folk core.

Nevertheless, we can categorize certain elements of Korean religious beliefs and practices as folk religion. For example, any belief or practice that appears to be indigenous to Korea, rather than a version of an imported form of spirituality such as Buddhism, Confucianism, or Christianity, can usually be labeled part of folk religion. Indigenous origins are usually considered one defining characteristic of folk religion. Another characteristic of a folk-religious belief or practice is that it is unique to a particular place or people. The lack of clearly defined doctrines or a well-defined institutional structure and hierarchy is another hallmark of folk religion. These are all characteristics of the traditional spiritual practices of the Korean people: animism and shamanism. Korean animism and shamanism have been have been so closely intertwined and so prevalent on the Korean peninsula for so long that most observers would say they form the original religion of Korea. They are often spoken of under the single term "shamanism," though they are actually quite different. Animism is based on the belief that inert objects such as mountains, trees, wind, and rain are inhabited by spirits that human beings can interact with. The term "animism" is applied to such beliefs because animists believe that even lifeless objects such as stones and stars are inhabited by spirits that are alive; thus, these objects are "animated." Animism can be found all over the world; however, because animism usually focuses its religious attention on the spirits of local natural objects and weather patterns, it is the quintessential local religion. The world of Korean animism is an enchanted world, in which spirits inhabit many of the natural objects Koreans encounter in their local environments, such as mountains and rivers. As conceived in Korea's folk religion, the natural world is not governed by impersonal forces operating according to laws of nature that operate independently of human will and behavior. Rather, it is a world endowed with willful personalities that must be cajoled, entertained, flattered, and bribed to act in ways beneficial to human beings. Many natural events, such as strong winds, are identified with spirits and deities and are credited to their deliberate activity. If rain does not fall when our crops need it, that indicates we have failed to perform those rituals that are necessary to convince the rain god to shower his favor on our fields. If someone in our household falls ill, that means we have failed to take the steps necessary to keep disease-bearing spirits at a distance. If our village fails to prosper, it is because we have not treated the village tutelary deity properly and have thus released that deity from his or her obligation to protect and assist us.

One of the ways we can convince spirits to work harmoniously with us is to talk to them. It is usually women, housewives and grandmothers, who converse with local spirits. They can sometimes be spotted standing before a shrine to a local god, bowing slightly while rapidly rubbing their hands together and asking that god for a favor. However, sometimes they ask a professional ritual specialist to intercede with the spirits on their behalf. In Korea's folk religion, those professional ritual specialists are shamans.

The difference between shamanism and animism is that shamanism is a method that human beings can use to interact with any god or spirit—not just those found in animism, but also deceased ancestors or deified heroes from the past, for example. Shamans become channels for human beings to contact a wide variety of invisible personalities. Shamanism, like animism, is found all over the world. However, because there is no shaman pope dictating how shamans should perform or even which gods they should interact with, shamans and their rituals differ dramatically from place to place and culture to culture. Korean shamans, the costumes they wear, the gods and spirits they interact with, and the rituals they perform are distinctive. No one watching a Korean shaman at work would confuse her with a Japanese, Chinese, Mongolian, or Siberian shaman. The Korean terms translated as "shaman" refer to three different types of ritual specialists. The best-known type of Korean shaman is the charismatic shaman, who is closest to the traditional meaning of that term outside of Korea. Outside the Korean peninsula, the appellation "shaman" is typically given to those who are able to contact the spirit world directly by going into a trance and leaving their body to embark on a spirit journey to the supernatural realm. Charismatic Korean shamans contact spirits via a different technique. Rather than traveling to meet those invisible beings, they have the spirits come to them. A charismatic shaman in Korea goes into a trance in order to be possessed by a spirit and then lets that spirit speak through her to members of her audience. Through her, Koreans are able to plead with spirits to stop afflicting them with physical, financial, or personal problems, or are able to talk once again with recently deceased loved ones. Charismatic shamans are the most dramatic representatives of Korean shamanism, and they are thriving in modern South Korea. Until recently, however, charismatic shamans were outnumbered by hereditary shamans. Hereditary shamans do not fit the usual definition of a shaman. They are ritual specialists who have inherited the power to perform certain rituals that influence the behavior of spirits, and they have also inherited a clientele—regular customers from their home village or from neighboring villages. However, hereditary shamans do not go into a trance, travel to the land of the spirits, or become possessed by spirits. Moreover, since they used to be ritual specialists for village communities, they have begun to disappear as modernization and urbanization have eliminated both the notion of hereditary occupations and the need for village-based ritual specialists.

A third type of shaman, more common in twenty-first-century Korea than hereditary shamans, are shamanic diviners. A diviner is someone who performs divination or fortune-telling; shamanic fortune-tellers read the words of the spirits in the throw of coins or rice grains. They normally do not experience spirit possession, nor do they perform the elaborate rituals other shamans perform. Instead, they sit in offices in Korea's cities and quietly offer advice to their customers based on their interpretation of signs from the spirits.

The vast majority of shamans in Korea, whether charismatic, hereditary, or divining, are women (they are not referred to as "shamanesses"), and most of their customers are women. People go to shamans seeking solutions to practical problems, such as family financial woes, worry over a daughter's marriage prospects or a son's chances of getting into a good university, or health problems within a family. A shaman's customers don't expect the sort of solemn religious ritual seen in many formal religious settings. If a person goes to see a shamanic diviner, she normally doesn't expect much more than a casual conversation about the problems she's facing and what

A charismatic shaman dancing to induce the trance required for possession by a spirit. She is wearing traditional male clothing above her waist and on her head, something such shamans often do during their rituals. Photo of shaman Jung Soon-duk taken by Kim Dongkyu.

the future may hold. However, a person who goes to a hereditary shaman will expect singing, dancing, and loud chanting. A hereditary shaman is expected to perform rituals that will compel the spirits to behave properly.

In addition to the singing, dancing, and chanting performed by a hereditary shaman, a charismatic shaman will also talk with the spirits and even argue with them in order to determine which spirit is bothering her client and why. She may become possessed by the spirit who is causing trouble so that the offended parties can talk to that spirit and convince it to change its behavior. (Bribery in the form of money presented to the shaman is a particularly effective way to change a wayward spirit's behavior.) Once a charismatic shaman has determined the cause of her client's problems, she may become possessed by a different spirit that will then order the offending spirit to treat the shaman's client better. The shaman may even threaten the offending spirit and force it to flee. In a full-scale ritual, a charismatic shaman may prove that she has been possessed by a spirit powerful enough to chastise other spirits by taking off her shoes and stepping barefooted onto the upright blades of two fodder-cutting knives.

Not all shamanic rituals require threats against spirits. Sometimes shamans perform rituals to thank spirits who have helped them predict the otherwise unpredictable, explain the unexplainable, and prevent the unpreventable. Some hereditary shamans perform rituals for the recently deceased in which they use friendly persuasion to help the dead move from this world to the next. Clients will come to a charismatic shaman to ask her to allow the spirit of a departed loved one to possess her so that family members may say things to the loved one they were not able to say before. For example, the family of someone who has died suddenly may ask the shaman's aid in saying appropriate farewells.

If a shaman is hereditary or charismatic—that is, as long as she is not a mere divining shaman—clients will expect a show. They expect the shaman to dress in brightly colored clothing, often wearing a costume like that of a powerful official from ages past. They also expect loud music played on drums and other percussion instruments. Such a show can be quite expensive. It used to be the case that those who were either unable or unwilling to spend large amounts of cash to win the cooperation of gods, spirits, and ancestors had a variety of less expensive ways to influence the behavior of invisible beings. Most notably, housewives could interact with household gods without the expensive intercession of a shaman. Until just a few decades ago, most Koreans lived in traditional thatch-roofed, clay-walled homes alongside dirt paths in villages or small towns. Those traditional homes were inhabited by a variety of spirits, including a god of the hearth, a god of the roof beam in the main room of the house, and even a god of the outhouse. It was the job of the housewife to maintain good relations with those various gods through informal rituals that did not require the presence of a shaman. Only on special occasions or when informal interaction with spirits appeared to have failed would a shaman be called in. However, most Koreans today live in concrete homes or high-rise condominium complexes along paved city streets. As Korea's traditional houses have begun to

disappear in the rush to urban modernity, so too have the gods who
dwelled in them and the rituals used to win their cooperation begun
to vanish. Household gods are an endangered species in modern Korea, but housewives are still held responsible for maintaining good
relations with gods and spirits in order to maintain wealth, health,
and happiness in the family. The disappearance of household gods
means they may have to use the services of a shaman more often than
they would have in the past. The housewife does not usually approach
shamans or the gods to make personal requests. Normally, she represents her family, because Korean spirituality places more emphasis
on the good of the group than on the wishes of the individual.

In the past, women were often given responsibility for official interaction with local spirits, even when that interaction took place at
the behest of a male-dominated government. The staunchly Confucian Chosŏn dynasty (1392–1910) in its early years sometimes called
upon shamans to pray for rain or to plead with spirits causing illness
in a member of the royal family, as did earlier dynasties. However,
there also were special occasions on which men rather than women
took the lead in interacting with local deities on behalf of their family
or their community. Until the second half of the twentieth century,
those occasions included village festivals.

Village festivals were an occasion for an entire village to come together once a year, usually at the beginning of a new year, to reaffirm
village solidarity and thank the tutelary deities for keeping the village safe and sound. Those tutelary deities in an inland agricultural
community would usually include the local mountain god as well as
a pair of spirit-generals—the male general of heaven and the female
general of the earth. The mountain god could normally be found
in a shrine on the hill behind the village. The two generals took the
form of totems that stood at the entrance to the village and kept harmful spirits away. (In fishing villages, the Dragon King who ruled the
waters might replace the mountain god as the main tutelary deity.)
Those gods are usually considered gods from Korea's folk pantheon,
yet the formal annual ritual thanking them and asking for their
continued help was often led by male village elders who performed
that ritual with the quiet dignity characteristic of Confucian rituals.

Some villages, however, would invite a female shaman to join them after the formal ritual and lead villagers in a livelier display of gratitude to the village's spiritual guardians. In other villages, the shaman would lead the primary ritual, but male village elders would be in charge of the preparations.

Another area of folk religiosity in which men played a significant role was the creation of lucky charms. These were pieces of paper on which powerful Chinese character phrases or graphic depictions of spiritual forces were drawn. They could be drawn and bestowed by a female shaman or by a male Buddhist monk, and they were considered to be equally effective against disease and ill fortune or in bringing good luck either way. We do not know the names of the artists who produced folk paintings of polka-dotted tigers that were believed to keep disease-bearing spirits at bay, but it is assumed that most if not all of them were men.

The urbanization of Korea has dramatically altered the ways in which Koreans interact with their local gods. The few village festivals that survive in South Korea today are held more as expressions of regional cultural pride (and a desire for tourist dollars) than as a manifestation of spirituality. Community folk religiosity is going the way of the household gods. The only element of Korea's folk religion that remains strong and viable in the twenty-first century is shamanism, particularly charismatic shamanism and shamanic divination. Koreans who seek supernatural help in overcoming the problems of life and who want to do so via intermediaries from the folk tradition can still hire a shaman.

A couple of other features of Korean folk religion have remained the same. Shamans continue to be almost all female, and housewives continue to bear the major responsibility for fruitful cooperation with invisible forces that can help them keep their family happy, healthy, and on the road to prosperity. Given the large number of gods dwelling in a traditional Korean home, that is not a simple task. It is easy for a housewife to inadvertently offend one or another of those gods and thus bring misfortune upon her family. In a modern house or condominium, there are not nearly as many deities to worry about, but there are still enough external deities—such as the deities overseeing small businesses or protecting new automobiles — to make it easy for a housewife to neglect or offend a spirit, who will then let her and her family feel its displeasure.

Even a housewife who feels that she has left premodern village traditions behind and has adopted instead the modern beliefs and values of Christianity may still be influenced by the assumptions of the folk religion, because those assumptions are so deeply embedded in Korean culture. The assumption that wives are more responsible than husbands for maintaining the family's harmonious relations with the spirit world may be one reason why women are much more likely than men to patronize a shaman, frequent a Buddhist temple, or attend a Christian church. They are trying to make sure they won't be accused of neglecting their spiritual duties to their family.

A core assumption of Korea's folk religion is that if things go wrong, it is because we have failed to properly manage our relationships with the spirits who have the ability to intervene in our lives. We bring trouble on ourselves when we act more as isolated individuals than as members of a community that embraces both visible and invisible beings. Such selfishness creates disharmony; and, as a result, we suffer. We do not suffer because those spirits are evil by nature, but rather because we have failed to maintain good relations with them, which will cause those powerful entities to ignore our wants and needs.

Sometimes the spirits cause problems even if we have done nothing to provoke them. The spirit of a recently deceased loved one may try to maintain contact with those he or she left behind. A dead grandfather, trying to reach beyond his grave to give a loving caress to a grandchild, may cause that grandchild to fall ill, because the touch of the dead is unhealthy for the living. The mother of that child is then supposed to contact the spirit of the deceased to remind him that he is dead and should accept his new place in the family order, rather than try to continue to interact with the living as he did while he was alive. A shaman will often be called in to relay that kind of message.

"Hungry ghosts" can also cause problems. Hungry ghosts are the spirits of those who died so young that they left no descendants behind to honor them after their death. Because they have no one to offer them the ritual food presented in ancestor memorial services, they are constantly hungry. This leads them to interfere with the affairs of the living in the hope that those still alive will notice their invisible presence and offer them the ritual food they crave. The only way to stop their interference is to find out who they are, provide them with the food they want, and then ask them to please go away. Such a task is best accomplished by a shaman. It is usually the housewife who decides whether or not it is necessary to summon a shaman.

Even though unhappy or confused spirits may be the immediate cause of many of the problems we face, those problems are ultimately our fault. (More precisely, in the folk religion it is usually the housewife's fault.) It is our fault because spirits only cause problems when we have failed to take the steps necessary to convince them to play their rightful role in our family, our village, or our country.

Statue and painting of a mountain god (with his tiger companion) in the mountain god shrine behind Yongsusa Buddhist Temple near the city of Andong, South Korea. Author photo.

Spirits, whether ancestral spirits, nature gods, or tutelary village deities, expect to be fed and entertained on a regular basis. Villages that neglect the annual festivals that are the standard way for villagers to thank their guardian deity for protection from disease, drought, or flooding can expect that protection to be withdrawn. Descendants who forget the last wishes of a departed relative can expect that relative to send unpleasant reminders, such as unexplained minor ailments, from beyond the grave. And households that don't maintain their relationship with their local mountain god might suffer financial reversals or health problems as a result.

The relationship between spirits and humans is similar to the relationship between one human being and another. People generally do not go out of their way to help someone who has ignored them or turned their back on them; spirits are the same. However, while failing to give spirits their due will have unpleasant consequences, such misbehavior is not considered a sin. In the worldview that prevails in Korea's folk religion, there are no sins, if sins are understood as actions contrary to the will of God. Instead, there are taboos and expectations. None of the gods in the folk pantheon issue commandments, but there are certain behavioral guidelines that regulate human interaction with a god or spirit. For example, before automobiles became common in Korea, shamans and other believers in the folk religion would regularly make pilgrimages on foot to the mountain shrines of patron deities. On such a pilgrimage, they were supposed to maintain silence on their way to and from the shrine in order to maintain the proper attitude of respect for the god they were visiting that day. Now that almost everyone has an automobile and paved roads can bring worshippers relatively close to their destination, such religious journeys are no longer a major undertaking, and they do not require the solemnity they once did. Nevertheless, those who wish to maintain a beneficial relationship with a local god are advised to continue paying regular visits to that god's shrine (even if they talk in the car as they drive there), bowing before the shrine to show respect and placing small gifts before the shrine as a sign of gratitude. Similarly, in a traditional home, the housewife is expected to occasionally leave a bowl of water or some rice cakes for her household gods.

Such expectations do not constitute commandments; they are more like rules of etiquette applied to interactions between human beings and spiritual beings. Unfortunately, Koreans are unable to consistently act so as to win the cooperation of the spirits, gods, and ancestors who share the universe with them, despite the fact that the Korean tradition states that human beings have the innate ability to be perfect. No matter how hard Koreans try to do what they think is right so that they can keep the spirits friendly and helpful, something will happen to show that at least some spirits are displeased. Rain won't fall, a loved one will fall ill, or a first child will be a daughter, indicating that they have somehow managed to fail to do what they were supposed to do. Even though they have shamans to help them placate the spirits who wield so much power over their lives, Koreans still have to endure disease and death, flood and famine, and the uncertainty and insecurity that are inescapable parts of the human condition. When misfortune befalls them, they feel guilty for not having done what they were supposed to have done, and ashamed because others in their family or their village can see that they have failed. It is not surprising, therefore, that Koreans began looking for a more effective way to gain some control over their lives. This is what made Koreans receptive to Buddhism, Confucianism, and Daoism when those Chinese forms of spirituality began entering the peninsula in the fourth century CE. Chinese spirituality offered the aid of supernatural beings, such as the Buddha, who were said to be more powerful than local deities. It also offered techniques for promoting harmony and pursuing sagehood, a goal clearly defined and explicitly promoted by Buddhism and Confucianism. Chinese spirituality gave Koreans hope that the dangers and uncertainties folk religion had failed to eliminate could be countered after all. By providing tools for reducing the uncertainties of life and therefore relieving those feelings of frustration—and even guilt and shame—that arose when things did not go as well as they should, Chinese religions and philosophies slowly began to gain a strong following on the peninsula.

CHAPTER 3

China's Three Teachings in Korea

Before the modern era, Korea did not have a specific term for religion as a separate and distinct form of human activity and organization. The Korean word that today means "religion" *(chonggyo)* was coined in Japan at the end of the nineteenth century. However, Korea recognized three "teachings" that it had imported from China beginning about one thousand five hundred years ago. Those three schools of thought and practice were treated by specialists (though not by most lay practitioners) as separate and distinct traditions. The names for those Three Teachings—Buddhism, Confucianism, and Daoism—function more as broad umbrella terms for clusters of philosophical and religious teachings, techniques, and practices than as designations for narrowly defined philosophical or religious orientations. In fact, there is so much variation within and among the traditions that sometimes it is hard to see how they can all fit in a single category called "religion." The term "Buddhism," for example, is used to refer to both a nontheistic philosophical Buddhism and a polytheistic popular Buddhism. The Confucian community included men devoted to self-cultivation as well as men primarily interested in political issues. And Daoism ranges from the iconoclastic sayings of Laozi and Zhuangzi to the pursuit of immortality by "internal alchemists."

These Three Teachings represented an approach to spirituality quite different from that represented by Korea's folk religion. For one thing, they took written texts seriously, as opposed to the folk religion, which was primarily an oral tradition. Buddhists relied on the words of the Buddha, as relayed through sutras, and on commentaries by revered monks from the past explaining those sutras. Confucians had their own set of revered writings, the ancient Confucian Classics, as well as commentaries on those Classics that were written much later. Daoists were less attached to a specific body of written works, but they read the *Daodejing* by Laozi, as well as the *Book of Changes* and Chinese texts describing techniques for enhancing longevity. In another contrast with Korea's folk tradition, the Chinese imports performed their rituals in large buildings erected specifically for that purpose. Buddhism is associated with temple complexes comprising several spacious wooden buildings; Confucianism has study halls, within which study takes on ritualistic overtones, and halls for enshrining great sages from the past. Daoism, though it had a much smaller institutional presence in Korea than did the other two religions, on occasion built ritual halls for use in government-sponsored rites. The folk tradition, however, does not build large temples. Often its sacred places are marked only by a pile of rocks along a mountain path or next to a sacred tree, or by a small shed holding a painted image of a local god. Its totem poles marking the presence of village guardian gods stood exposed to the weather outside the entrance to the village, rather than inside a great hall as statues of buddhas or tablets honoring Confucius usually did.

The three new religions also brought with them a new notion of a clearly defined administrative and liturgical hierarchy, along with specified procedures for legitimizing the status of their professional practitioners and specialists. There was nothing in the folk religion comparable to a Buddhist monk, who left his family and abandoned his traditional clothing for monks' robes and a small room in a monastery. Nor did shamans have to pass the written examinations that provided the degrees that identified a man as a Confucian scholar. Even the professional Daoist priests in Korea (when there were any) were full-time civil servants, unlike shamans who were sometimes at the beck and call of the government but spent most of their time working among villagers and fisherfolk.

The initiation ceremony of a charismatic shaman is also dramatically different from the ordination of a Buddhist monk or the awarding of an academic degree to a Confucian scholar. Buddhists and Confucians follow standardized procedures, and their rituals recognizing professional status are solemn affairs. Shamanic initiation rituals, on the other hand, are a noisy mixture of oral tradition and spontaneity. In the case of charismatic shamans, the initiate is required to display her new status by speaking the unscripted words of her particular patron spirit. If she is unable to show that she has actually been possessed during the ritual, she will not be recognized as a legitimate shaman.

One more significant difference between the new teachings from China and the folk religion of Korea is that the Three Teachings all have explicit definitions of what we may call a sage (although the Sino-Korean characters representing that concept differed among the three traditions). In Buddhism, sages are those who have completely activated their inner Buddha nature and who thus think and act in accordance with it. In Confucianism, sages are those who have revitalized their innate ability to rise above self-absorption, allowing them to view the world objectively and act accordingly. For internal alchemy Daoists, sages are human beings who have transformed themselves into mountain immortals, free from the constraints of ordinary physical existence. Although these conceptions of sagehood are more salient in the philosophical versions of these traditions than in the religious versions that focus more on immediate practical benefits, the sage still loomed larger in China's Three Teachings than in Korea's folk religion. Korea's shamans are not sages in any Buddhist, Confucian, or Daoist sense of the term. They are merely individuals who are particularly skilled at contacting and influencing invisible beings in order to help others achieve their goals.

Buddhism

The first of the Three Teachings to have a dramatic impact on Korean spirituality was Buddhism, even though it had a shorter history in China than the other two. When Buddhism first entered Korea, in the late fourth century CE, it took the guise of a more powerful form of the folk religion. Korea's first Buddhist monks performed miracles that suggested that the Buddha could heal diseases that the less powerful gods of the folk religion could not. However, those first miracles were not performed to answer housewives' prayers or to relieve them of frustration or assuage their guilt. Instead, those displays of the Buddha's healing power occurred within the palaces of Korea's first kingdoms. Buddhism was brought to those palaces by Chinese and central Asian monks who promised Korea's emerging royal families that Buddhism could help them stay healthy, as well as helping them solidify and centralize their authority. From the fourth through the seventh centuries, three kingdoms fought for control of the Korean peninsula, and the rulers of those kingdoms were interested in any tool that would give them a competitive advantage over their rivals. The first kingdom to adopt Buddhism was Koguryŏ, in 372. Two decades later, the king of Koguryŏ proclaimed to his subjects, "Let us reap benefits by respecting and trusting the Buddhist Way." Shortly afterward, Koguryŏ embarked on one of the most successful military campaigns in Korean history, capturing (according to a stele erected in 414) fifty-four walled towns and one thousand four hundred villages. Silla was the weakest of the three kingdoms until it too embraced Buddhism, in 528. Less than a century and a half later, Silla defeated both Koguryŏ and Paekche to become the dominant power on the peninsula.

Buddhism acquired its power to enhance political authority through its doctrine of karma, which stated that the actions people took and the desires they entertained in the past determined what happened to them in the present and the future. The notion of karma was relatively easy for Koreans to accept, because it reinforced their pre-Buddhist assumption that human beings are personally responsible for whatever problems they face. Kings listened carefully when monks told them that if they sponsored the construction of temples and supported the monks who lived in them, they would show that they were concerned for more than just their individual self-interest. By thus rising above self-absorption, they would accumulate good karma and counteract bad karma. More good karma meant fewer problems with their enemies. Therefore, the way to build a powerful kingdom was to support Buddhism. This explanation for the benefits derived from sponsoring temples was reinforced by an addendum provided by the monk Tosŏn in the ninth century. Temples, according to Tosŏn, could redirect the energy that flowed through invisible underground channels so that those who lived above ground could derive more benefit from it.

This is worldly Buddhism. It doesn't display much influence from the Four Noble Truths, which are the original core teachings of Buddhism. The first Korean converts to Buddhism, however, didn't seem particularly interested in the Noble Truth that suffering is inevitable because we desire what we can never have. Nor were they particularly interested in cultivating the cessation of desire that is supposed to be the solution to suffering. Instead, they adopted Buddhism because they were persuaded that it could help them gain what they desired, such as health, longevity, and greater political stability and power.

Later, Koreans began to see that Buddhism also addressed the apparent contradiction of inappropriate thought and behavior in human beings, who were believed to be essentially good. As Buddhism became established on the Korean peninsula and as Korean monks began to read the Buddhist sutras carefully, some began to understand that there was more to Buddhism than access to more supernatural power than folk religion could provide. Among those who pioneered a deeper understanding of the teachings of Buddhism was the monk Wǒnhyo (617–686).

Wǒnhyo was just one of several monks in the sixth and seventh centuries who moved beyond the notion of Buddhism as primarily a political and medical tool. Many of those monks traveled to China or even as far as India to obtain copies of sutras and learn how to interpret them. Though Wǒnhyo never left Korea, he become one of the most prolific Korean commentators on the sutras, producing more than eighty titles in which he analyzed and harmonized the arguments of various competing schools of Buddhist philosophy and practice in China. Outside Korea, he is best known for what is probably an apocryphal tale of his enlightenment.

Wǒnhyo is said to have been on a journey when it grew too dark for him to walk any farther, so he retired to a nearby cave for the night. During the night, he woke up thirsty and reached out for what he thought was refreshing spring water. He quenched his thirst and went back to sleep. When the sunlight awoke him the next morning, he discovered that the water he had so enjoyed the night before, thinking it was fresh spring water, was actually water that had collected inside a human skull. He noticed, to his surprise, that when he had thought the water came from a spring, it tasted fine; but when he saw that it came from a skull, it was disgusting. Wǒnhyo then realized that what we believed something to be was more important than what it actually was. This was how he became enlightened to the Buddhist teaching that we suffer because we impose our own perceptions, assumptions, and expectations on the world we experience. The ignorance that results is the cause of our inability to consistently think and act appropriately. Enlightenment, however, allows us to recover our innate goodness and eliminate the inappropriate thoughts and behavior that cause suffering.

Wŏnhyo represents philosophical Buddhism, which is less interested in asking various buddhas for specific favors in this world than in learning why this world will always disappoint us and how we can rise above the anguish that results from that disappointment. The philosophical approach to Buddhism shows little interest in interaction with gods and spirits; it is more concerned with understanding why human beings suffer and how we can stop suffering, and it focuses on ways to overcome the limitations of existence as an individual by realizing our own true Buddha nature, a realization that dissolves the harmful misperception that our existence as isolated, separate, distinct individuals defines what we are.

Philosophical Buddhism teaches that ignorance leads us to expect more from the phenomenal world than it can provide. We expect the things of this world to be long-lasting, so that if we enjoy something one day, it will be there for us to enjoy again the next. But friends move away, loved ones die, we lose a well-paying job, and our bodies begin to ache as we grow old. Everything in the world as we experience it will change sooner or later. However, it is not change per se that makes suffering an inescapable part of life; rather, we are disappointed and suffer because of our own ignorant expectation of permanence from a world in which everything is impermanent. Therefore, to eliminate suffering, we need to eliminate such ignorance and the desire for permanence that it generates. For Wŏnhyo, the best way to eliminate ignorance was to study Buddhist texts in order to learn from them the true nature of human consciousness and the world of experience it generates and interacts with. From those texts, we will learn that behind the world of experience and its ever-changing multiplicity of events and entities, there is an underlying undifferentiated and unchanging emptiness that is also pure thusness. Once we are enlightened to this infinite Buddha nature, we recognize that the world of everyday experience is only temporary, and we therefore will no longer make demands of the phenomenal world that it cannot meet.

By the ninth century, Wŏnhyo's intellectual approach to Buddhist enlightenment had been joined by the meditative approach known as Chan in China and Zen in Japan. Known as Sŏn in Korea, this variety of Buddhism teaches that we will remain ignorant, and therefore will continue to suffer, as long as we try to understand the world rather than rise above it. Understanding entails analysis, which requires dividing the world of experience into separate and distinct processes and entities. But, Sŏn says, it is precisely the mistaken imposition of plurality on a world that is essentially undifferentiated thusness that gives rise to impossible expectations. We should, therefore, turn off the analytical activity of our mind through the calming process of meditation.

In bringing cessation to suffering, proper meditation can also solve the problem of reincarnation. Philosophical Buddhists want to escape that cycle of birth, death, and rebirth, because rebirth brings us back into the world of transitory phenomena that will once again cause us to suffer. They argue that we return to this world because of our mistaken belief that our existence as an individual is real, rather than just a transitory phenomenon. (In Buddhist philosophy, only something permanent, unchanging, and uncaused is truly real.) When our body dies, if our mind is deluded by the illusion that we nevertheless remain a distinct individual, we seek to return to live in this world as an individual. That desire for continued existence causes us to be reborn and therefore to suffer again.

However, Buddhism teaches that individual existence is never permanent. Once we recognize this fact and accept the inevitability of change, we will no longer expect to be reborn. This realization will set us free. When we die, we can return to undifferentiated thusness. We will have entered nirvana, the end of existence as a separate and distinct individual, and we will not have to suffer anymore. In the meantime, if we are truly aware that our belief in our own individual existence is misleading, then we will not expect our individualistic desires to be satisfied and therefore will not be disappointed when they are not. We can transcend our limitations as an individual by recognizing that existence as an individual is not true existence.

Philosophical Buddhism did not appeal to the average person, for a couple of reasons. First of all, most people didn't have the time to spend years studying abstruse Buddhist texts explaining the nature of consciousness and the illusory nature of transitory phenomena. Nor did the average person have the time or the discipline to still their analytical mind so that they stopped thinking of themselves as individual human beings. Only those who left the responsibilities of everyday life for the isolation of a monastery had enough time to engage in the study and meditation that philosophical Buddhism seemed to demand.

Furthermore, most people were more interested in satisfying desires than in eliminating them. The extinction of individual existence in nirvana was less appealing than the possibility of long-term bliss after death in some kind of paradise. Learning to accept disappointment through lowered expectations was not as comforting as overcoming suffering by being cured of an illness, harvesting a bumper crop, or watching children grow into adults and bear healthy grandchildren.

Before Buddhism could gain the allegiance of significant portions of the general Korean population, it had to convince them that it could provide the same immediate and practical benefits the folk religion promised, and that it could do so more effectively and consistently than folk religion could. In other words, it had to present itself as being able to teach some Koreans how to eliminate ignorance and extinguish desires while at the same time teaching others how to satisfy desires before they were extinguished.

Religious Buddhism made its case in a number of ways. First, as an organized religion relying heavily on written texts and institutional memories, it was able to provide exact instructions for performing rituals as well as specific guidelines for determining who could be trusted to perform them. With trained Buddhist monks available, there would be no more need to go searching for a shaman who was particularly skilled at interacting with supernatural beings. In addition, religious Buddhism promised that its rituals were more effective at maintaining harmony in the cosmos than any of the rituals shamans performed. Some of those rituals involved chanting sacred phrases that were presented as being more efficacious than any words of the spirits that shamans could utter. Other rituals invoked the aid of Buddhist deities that were said to be more powerful than any of the gods and spirits of folk religion.

Unlike philosophical Buddhism, which focused on Sakyamuni Buddha as a teacher who offered advice on how to end suffering, religious Buddhism focused on various buddhas who intervened in human affairs in response to specific requests for supernatural assistance. The more popular buddhas since the Three Kingdoms period have included Amitabha (the buddha who presides over the Western Paradise), Maitreya (the buddha of the future), and Bhaishajyaguru (the Healing Buddha). Religious Buddhism also made appeals to bodhisattvas, celestial beings on the verge of perfect buddhahood who have postponed admission to nirvana until all other sentient beings can also be saved. A particularly popular bodhisattva is Avalokitesvara (the bodhisattva of compassion).

Each of these beings, in its own way, offers hope to those looking for concrete solutions to specific problems. The Amitabha Buddha (K. Amit'abul) recognizes how difficult it is for human beings to achieve insight into the true nature of consciousness, insight that philosophical Buddhism implies is necessary to win release from suffering. Feeling compassion for the many who could never achieve such a lofty goal in this world, Amitabha promises that he will allow anyone who places their trust in him to be reborn in paradise, where perfect insight will be easier to acquire. The promises of the Healing Buddha (K. Yaksa yŏraebul) are more concrete. He promises to heal all those who trust in him and who also display that trust through certain specified ritual displays of devotion. Maitreya (K. Milŭk) offers hope that a paradise will soon be established on this earth, though in the meantime believers can ask Maitreya to help them add a healthy son to their family or bestow health, wealth, and longevity on petitioners and their family members. The bodhisattva Avalokitesvara, known in Korea as Kwanŭm, "She Who Listens to the Cries of Humanity," is available for solving any problem a human being might face. She is sometimes depicted with several arms, the better to help a multitude of human beings in a multitude of ways at the same time. Two of her sutras, the *Heart Sutra* and the *Thou-*

Avalokitesvara, the bodhisattva of compassion, at Kaeunsa in Seoul.
Photo courtesy of Steven H. Lee.

sand Hands Sutra, are particularly beloved by Koreans and are often chanted in Buddhist rituals.

Cultivating insight into the true nature of reality and beseeching Buddhist deities for assistance were not the only things religious Buddhists did to gain release from suffering. They also strove to act properly. Buddhist instructions for proper behavior, as interpreted by philosophical Buddhists, are not a list of "commandments" in the sense of rules handed down from on high. Instead, Buddhism provides precepts—guidelines for avoiding thoughts and actions that reinforce the mistaken focus on the self that pulls human beings back after death to live and suffer again in this world of transitory and frustrating phenomena. The Buddha does not punish those who violate those precepts. Rather, according to the doctrine of karma, violators punish themselves by burrowing deeper into the soil of this world of selfish desires, immersing themselves in cravings that can never be completely satisfied. If, on the other hand, they follow the guidelines those precepts provide, they will leave behind their attachment to petty, transient pleasures and escape the trap created by their own deluded pursuit of self-interest. Philosophical Buddhism interprets the precepts of Buddhism as showing the way to earn the reward of release from the cycle of birth-death-rebirth that prolongs human suffering.

The devotional Buddhism that is more popular among the average lay believer also promises rewards for appropriate behavior and punishments for inappropriate behavior. However, popular devotional Buddhism envisions the recently departed appearing before ten different judges over the course of the forty-nine days that follow death. Depending on how the departed thought and behaved while they were alive, those judges might condemn them to reincarnation in one of several realms of horrendous suffering called "hells" or reward them with elevation to a trouble-free existence in the paradise called the Pure Land. Though this Pure Land strain of Buddhism was not as strong institutionally in Korea as it was in China or Japan, some temples in Korea have paintings on their walls depicting the torments that await those who violate the Buddhist precepts, in order to encourage those who visit that temple to behave appropriately. Moreover, all large Buddhist temple complexes in Korea include a Judgment Hall where the relatives and friends of the recently deceased can pray that the ten judges of the afterlife will be lenient with those who appear before them.

The most basic precepts of Buddhism are the five abstentions. Buddhists are told they should abstain from harming living beings, from taking things that do not belong to them, from engaging in inappropriate sexual activity, from lying or otherwise harming others with words they utter, and from clouding their minds with excessive use of alcohol or other mind-altering substances. Buddhists are also enjoined to think and act with generosity and compassion. In the Mahayana tradition of Buddhism that Koreans adopted, lay Buddhists as well as monks are encouraged to take the bodhisattva vow to dedicate themselves to helping all sentient beings. That can mean being willing to postpone their own release from this realm of suffering until all sentient beings can be released, but it can also mean helping the ill, the poor, and the disadvantaged in this life. The bodhisattva ideal of selfless generosity and compassion is such a core concept in Korean Buddhism that dedicated adult female practitioners, of the sort sometimes seen preparing meals in temple kitchens for monks to enjoy, are often addressed as *posallim* (honorable bodhisattva).

Believing that the goal of release from suffering can be reached through different paths, Korean Buddhists, like Buddhists in China and elsewhere, embraced what may appear to be contradictory approaches in the hope that at least one of those techniques, or a combination of them, might work. In Korea's major monasteries, for example, there are halls for worship as well as halls for sutra study and halls for meditation. Monks who meditate and study Buddhist philosophy will also lead congregations in an hour of bowing and chanting the name of Amitabha or of another buddha or bodhisattva. The great philosopher-monk Wŏnhyo is as well known for teaching peasants to chant the name of Amitabha Buddha to earn rebirth in paradise as for his philosophical commentaries on the sutras.

Monks who teach the renunciation of desire will welcome the faithful who hike up a mountain to bow repeatedly before a statue of Kwanŭm carved into a cliff near the summit and pray that the first child of their newly married daughter will be a boy. Those same monks will encourage, rather than discourage, those who want to offer monetary donations to a temple in return for a promise that a monk will pray for one hundred consecutive days that their eldest son will be accepted into one of Korea's top universities. Nor does Korea's Buddhist community exclude those who add pebbles to the small mounds of pebbles in and around temple grounds as a sign of their faith that the buddhas and bodhisattvas will grant their requests for health, wealth, longevity, or a male heir.

Korean Buddhism, like Chinese Buddhism, is sometimes labeled "syncretic" because it combines meditation and philosophical sutra study with religious practices such as prayers to Kwanŭm and the chanting of Amitabha's name. Such a broad embrace of both philosophical and religious spirituality is a sign that, for Koreans, the goal is often more important than the means used to reach that goal. The goal of Korean spirituality is overcoming the limitations of existence as an individual. Most Koreans believe that is accomplished by making connections with invisible forces more powerful than they are. Whether those invisible forces were Buddhist deities or should be better understood as the undifferentiated, all-encompassing thusness called Buddha nature was less important than the transcendence of individual limitations effected by linking with those forces.

Some Koreans, however, grew dissatisfied with Buddhism, despite the wide variety of spiritual practices it provided. They turned instead to another Chinese import in search of a way to transcend the limitations of existence as an individual.

Confucianism

When Buddhism first entered Korea, Confucianism came with it, as did Daoism. The Three Teachings were treated as part and parcel of the advanced civilization of China, comrades of each other rather than rivals. At first, Confucianism did not offer much in the way of spiritual guidance. Like Buddhism, it was first adopted by the ruling elite as a tool for governing; unlike Buddhism, it did not offer supernatural assistance to Korea's emerging kingdoms. Instead, Confucianism provided models for government organization and for the drafting of government documents and the keeping of government records. Koreans learned from Confucianism how to imitate China's bureaucratic approach to government.

Confucianism also reinforced ethical principles that are useful in maintaining an orderly society under the control of a centralized government. A core assumption of Confucianism is that if people learn to be loyal to their rulers, filial to their parents, deferential to their older siblings, correct in their relations with their spouses, and honest with their friends, then conflicts will be minimized and harmonious cooperation will prevail. Moreover, if everyone plays their assigned roles within the social hierarchy, accepting the responsibilities of a beneficiary toward a benefactor as well as acting as a benefactor toward appropriate beneficiaries, then society can effectively work toward the collective good.

For example, the proper ethical relationship between father and son was governed by love. In the case of the father, that love was manifested as paternal concern. A good father would ensure that his son had sufficient food, housing, clothing, and an education while he was young and would also provide proper moral guidance to his son both when he was a child and after he grew into adulthood. A son, on the other hand, was obligated to display his love through filial piety toward his father. That meant that he should obey and respect his father; should marry and sire a son to carry on the family line; should take care of his father when his father grew old and frail; and, after his father passed away, should show through proper, regular ritual displays of devotion that he had not forgotten his father and was still grateful for all he had done for him. A filial son would perform similar ritual displays of gratitude to those who gave his father life, such as his father's father, his father's grandfather, and so on.

The specifics of how that filial piety is to be demonstrated have changed over the centuries. In the first part of the twentieth century, a son showed that he respected his father by refraining from smoking in front of him and by not wearing sunglasses in his father's presence. The eldest son was also expected to live with his father and mother, even as an adult, so that he and his wife could take care of them when they had worked long enough to deserve to be taken care of by others. The expectations for proper filial conduct have loosened somewhat in recent decades. Smoking and wearing sunglasses are no longer as strictly proscribed. Some eldest sons have left their parents behind and emigrated overseas, and others who remained in Korea have moved into urban apartments too small to share with their parents. Still, most Korean sons, especially eldest sons, provide financial support for elderly parents and try to spend time with their parents on important family occasions, such as the Autumn Harvest Festival *(chusŏk)* and their parents' sixtieth and seventieth birthdays.

Perhaps the most striking legacies of the Confucian moral code in Korea today are the continuing emphasis on the production of male offspring to keep the father's family name alive, and the continued use of ritual to show respect for deceased parents and grandparents. These two filial obligations are related. During Korea's long Chosŏn dynasty, only males in a direct line of descent were permitted to lead memorial services for departed ancestors. That tradition has survived into the twenty-first century. In most Korean families today, although a daughter keeps the family name of her father as her surname even after she marries, she normally cannot lead the memorial services for her deceased parents or grandparents. Moreover, her children will usually take her husband's family name. Therefore, without a son to carry it on, the family name will disappear within two generations. Even worse, there will be no one who can organize and lead the memorial services necessary to keep the memory of ancestors alive and to provide visual reminders that their descendants continue to appreciate all the ancestors did for them.

Along with filial piety, the Confucian moral code also required loyalty to political authority. A ruler was supposed to be paternalistic, protecting those he ruled over from violence, crime, and excessive taxation. In return, the ruled were supposed to show their appreciation to their ruler with loyalty, obeying his commands and withholding support from any who might challenge him. Though such expectations of loyalty seem more appropriate for the monarchy that Korea was in premodern times than for the modern world, unquestioning loyalty remains a moral imperative in North Korea today. Moreover, the notion that loyalty is owed to superiors remained strong enough in South Korea to delay full democratization until the 1990s. In the mid-1970s, after South Korean president Park Chung Hee abandoned even the pretense of freely contested presidential elections, he promoted what he called a "new mind movement," a revival of the traditional Korean values of filial piety, loyalty, and propriety, in order to provide ideological support for his regime. Few questioned his claim that loyalty was a core Korean value, though some were bold enough to assert that the nation as a whole, not an individual ruler or government, was the proper object of such loyalty.

Another key Confucian value, one that also continues to influence Korean behavior today, is the injunction to elevate males over females in the public arena. Traditionally, that arena was supposed to include family life, because one of the five major human relationships was the one between a husband and a wife, and that conjugal relationship was supposed to be governed by a respect for gender differences in roles and responsibilities. Husbands were supposed to guide their wives, and wives were supposed to obey and support their husbands. Whether such gender inequality actually prevails in Korean homes today, or whether it even prevailed in all homes in the past, is open to question. What is clear to any observer of contemporary Korea is that patriarchy remains strong outside the home. South Korea has one of the lowest percentages of elected women officials of any industrialized country. Men dominate the business world as well as the pulpit; there are few female CEOs and even fewer female pastors in Korea's churches.

Confucianism is often criticized today for promoting a hierarchical society in contradiction of the modern belief that all human beings deserve to be treated equally. However, Confucians would counter that harmony is more important than equality. They believe that harmony is achieved when everyone accepts a division of roles and responsibilities, and the accompanying differences in status, within their families and communities. Confucians insisted that, human nature being what it is, such acquiescence normally would be instinctive, a spontaneous result of respect and appreciation for those who lead others, whether they are parents or community leaders. Confucian moral obligations were not seen as inhibiting normal human behavior but rather were understood as natural expressions of gratitude to those who have helped make us what we are.

In addition to teaching such communitarian values, Confucianism also promoted rituals intended to help transcend the limitations of individuality. Among the earliest Confucian Classics are ritual handbooks that provided detailed instructions for how particular rituals should be enacted. Participants in a ritual, no matter their individual preferences, had to interact with other participants in certain specified ways. That meant they acted as part of a larger community (in this case, the community of participants in that ritual) rather than acting as unique individuals. They were not allowed to do whatever they wanted to do; instead, ritual performers had to focus on the roles they were assigned in the ritual. A groom, for example, had to act the way any man getting married would act on that special day. A grieving son had to mourn his parents the way his parents had mourned their parents, and the way his sons would mourn him. Proper ritual performance thus encouraged participants to turn their gaze away from their individuality and focus on the positions they held in their community.

Etiquette, the rituals of everyday interpersonal interaction, had the same moral intent. Confucian etiquette requires men and women to remain aware at all times of the relative social status of the persons with whom they are interacting. They are supposed to show respect for those above them while being considerate of those beneath them. According to the Confucian norms of politeness, young people should defer to their elders, students should use courteous language when talking to their teachers, and women should speak more softly than men in public and walk a step behind them.

Modern men and women often find Confucian etiquette stifling. Many of us today reject the Confucian assumption that harmony is more important than equality. Twenty-first-century men and women also increasingly repudiate the supposition that age or gender should determine the roles people play. Nevertheless, we cannot overlook the appeal Confucianism had for Koreans in premodern times and still has for some Koreans today. In a society governed by strict Confucian protocol, individual behavior would be more predictable, easing one of the sources of uncertainty, tension, and conflict in life. Even today that lessening of tension and conflict is reason enough, in the eyes of some, to accept the Confucian code of conduct. Furthermore, Confucian etiquette requires that everyone treat each other politely, regardless of where they are on the social ladder. For those who bemoan the lack of civility in modern life, Confucianism provides a possible corrective, especially if it is modified to take into account the contemporary recognition that women deserve the same respect that traditional Confucianism accorded men.

For the first few centuries that Confucianism was on the Korean peninsula, it usually accepted a division of responsibility with Buddhism. Confucianism taught how to behave in everyday life, both in the family and in government, while Buddhism offered supernatural assistance for intractable problems and provided metaphysical explanations of the nature of reality. This limited role for Confucianism began to change at the end of Korea's Koryŏ kingdom (918–1392). In the Chosŏn kingdom that replaced Koryŏ, Confucianism replaced Buddhism as the form of spirituality favored by the state and by the ruling elite.

The importance of Confucianism in Korean spirituality began to change in the fourteenth century, because Confucianism itself had changed. A couple of centuries earlier in China, a new form of Confucianism had appeared. Known to Westerners as Neo-Confucianism, this more philosophical Confucianism represented an assertion of the ultimate importance of Confucian moral principles in the face of the Buddhist claim that nothing that was of this world was truly real. Neo-Confucianism turned on its head the Buddhist belief that anything that changes is somehow less real than something that is permanent and unchanging. For Neo-Confucianism, it is precisely change that is real because reality itself is constituted by patterns of change. Neo-Confucian spirituality, like Buddhism, seeks to transcend individuality, but not by linking with undifferentiated thusness; rather, Neo-Confucianism believes that we can transcend individuality by playing our proper role within the patterns of appropriate interaction in a constantly changing universe.

For example, Neo-Confucians argued that Buddhist monks were immoral because they renounced their responsibilities to their families and fled into mountain monasteries to pursue personal enlightenment. Monks also left behind the land they were supposed to farm and from which the government expected to collect taxes. Their behavior, in Neo-Confucian eyes, was selfish; Buddhist monks placed their own happiness above the needs of the larger community. Truly moral persons would obey their parents and would take care of them when they were old, not abandon them for a monastic life. Those who did so placed an unfair share of the responsibility for taking care of their parents on their brothers and sisters. Nor would moral subjects abandon their fields, because in so doing, they made others pay additional taxes to make up for the taxes that monks didn't pay.

In the Neo-Confucian worldview, the world around us and our relationships with it are constantly changing. Our job is to take note of those changes and then alter our behavior to adapt to those changes. It is immoral to try to avoid change by fleeing the world. The fact that we will feel sad when a loved one eventually dies is no reason to leave them while they are still alive. The fact that we don't want to worry about whether we will get enough rain for our fields is no reason to abandon agriculture for sutra study, prayer, and meditation. Families and communities need every member to play their assigned roles. Someone who doesn't play his or her role, even if they have "spiritual" reasons for doing so, is like someone who removes a spoke from a wheel. If enough spokes are removed, the wheel collapses. Neo-Confucianism insists that we should think about the effect of our actions on our family and our society, and always act with the greater good in mind rather than our personal self-interest. To meet the Buddhist challenge, Neo-Confucianism had to do more than merely criticize Buddhist behavior as immoral. It also had to offer a vision of the universe in which Confucian values were real and the Buddhist perspective was mistaken. In addition, it had to provide techniques for overcoming the limitations of existence as an individual. Neo-Confucians began by asserting that the world of human experience was real. It was not created by our ignorant minds, as Buddhist philosophers claimed, but by the interaction of *li* and *ki*. *Ki* (C. *qi*) is the basic stuff, both matter and energy, out of which the universe is formed. As such, it is the primary reason there are separate and distinct entities in the cosmos. I am different from you because my *ki*, my physical composition, is different from your *ki*.

Li, on the other hand, is the Neo-Confucian name for the unifying pattern of appropriate interactions that defines the world humans experience. Often misleadingly translated as "principle," *li* is much more active than that term implies. *Li* integrates the various bits of *ki* in the universe into a dynamic pattern of cooperation. Moreover, specific manifestations of *li* determine which specific roles each person and object plays at any particular point in time. For example, it is the *li* of a student to study, just as it is the *li* of a child to obey his or her parents. However, a student could grow up to be a teacher, at which point he should follow the *li* of a teacher and act like a teacher rather than like a student. A child will grow up to be a parent and should then follow the *li* of a parent, acting like a parent rather than like a child. Against the Buddhist doctrine that changing things are unreal because they are unstable, Neo-Confucians insisted that everything that is real is in a constant state of flux. Our job as members of a family, subjects of a king, and inhabitants of the universe is to determine what our changing roles are within the constantly changing network of patterns of interaction that constitutes the cosmos, and then act accordingly. In other words, we should study the patterns of change in order to become a sage. Neo-Confucian prescriptions for sagehood were designed to allow *li,* which not only defines the universe but also constitutes our essential human nature, to shine through our *ki* and direct our behavior. *Ki,* as the individualizing force in the cosmos, tends to direct our thoughts and actions toward what will benefit us personally. However, we are born with a virtuous nature, and if we cultivate that innate tendency toward cooperation, it will direct us toward appropriate patterns of interaction. How do we cultivate our innate goodness? Ritual and etiquette are one way. Ritual and etiquette force us to put personal preferences aside and instead perform whatever roles are appropriate for us to perform in the specific interpersonal relationships in which we find ourselves. The study of the Confucian Classics is another way to cultivate the appropriate *li.* Neo-Confucians respected wise men from the past and believed that those sages knew what *li* was and tried to pass that knowledge on to later generations. By studying what the sages wrote, we too can learn to recognize *li.* Because knowledge and action were believed to be intimately connected, Neo-Confucians assumed that once we know what *li* is, we will act in accordance with it.

A third approach to cultivating attitudes and actions that conform to *li* is the "investigation of things," the Neo-Confucian term for observation of patterns of change in the external world. Observing the world around us on its own terms is a way to cultivate the key Neo-Confucian virtue of sincerity. Sincerity, as Neo-Confucians defined it, means thinking and acting without concern for what benefits us personally. Observing patterns of appropriate interaction in the external world was believed to be an effective technique for countering the self-absorption that can taint attempts to view the world from an unselfish point of view. The things Neo-Confucians investigated could include the writings of the Confucian sages and reports by historians of appropriate and inappropriate behavior in the past. Things to be investigated could also include poetry and music, as well as invisible patterns of energy in the earth and the movements of celestial objects in the heavens above.

Though feng shui, also known misleadingly as geomancy, is usually associated with Daoism in the West, in premodern Korea it was an integral part of the Confucian worldview. Confucian scholars en-

*The Hall of Respect for Righteousness in the Nokdong Sŏwŏn Confucian
Academy near Taegu. Author photo.*

deavored to identify the invisible streams of *ki* flowing through the
earth so they could identify the best hillside location for burying
their parents and the best location in or near their village to build
their home. They believed that *ki* flowing through the bones of ancestors would be translated into energy that could make their descendants healthy and wealthy. They also believed that a house built in or
near a spot with an abundance of life-giving energy would allow the
members of the family living in that house to enjoy long and pros-
perous lives. Such attention to the possible benefits of linking up with
the *ki* of the earth was not seen as self-interested behavior. Instead, it
was praised as one way to interact properly with the natural world by
harmonizing human actions above ground with natural patterns of
movement below ground.

    Similarly, astronomers scanned the skies for any signs of unusual
celestial phenomena, such as an unpredicted eclipse or the sudden

appearance of a comet. Such departures from the normal patterns of movement in the heavens were reported to Confucian officials, who interpreted them as evidence that human behavior had disturbed the harmonious operation of the universe. They believed such anomalies were warnings that they should rectify their behavior to eliminate any pursuit of their own self-interest at the expense of the common good.

Another important guide to proper behavior was the *Book of Changes*. Confucian scholars believed that the *Book of Changes* identified sixty-four basic patterns of change in the cosmos. Certain techniques, such as throwing six *yut* sticks (which were round on one side and flat on the other) onto a table and seeing which ones landed on the flat side and which ones landed on the round side, could reveal which pattern was dominant at that time and in which direction it was changing. Calculating which pattern was dominant and which one was on its way to dominance on the hour, day, month, and year of a person's birth (the so-called "four pillars" of destiny) would tell a person which cosmic patterns governed his life. Such techniques allowed a Confucian scholar to align his actions with the patterns of change directing the universe. Harmonizing individual actions with cosmic patterns of change was one way to overcome the distortions introduced by considerations of narrow personal self-interest.

In every case, Confucian scholars encouraged the investigation of things not as a way to learn more about things per se, but as a way to overcome dangerous self-interest. Another way Confucian scholars tried to curb an excessive focus on personal benefit was to meditate. Neo-Confucian meditators did not attempt to imitate Buddhists by stilling their minds; instead, they sat and quietly observed their mind before it responded to external stimuli and then tried to cultivate tendencies to cooperate and work toward the common good while stilling emotions that represented desires for personal gain or pleasure.

Those who engaged in Neo-Confucian meditation were supposed to cultivate an attitude of reverence. To Neo-Confucians, that term implies respect for the universe as a whole and for all of its component elements and the roles they play. A reverent attitude will produce a sincere will. Someone who is sincere will put aside consider-ations of what is best for them as an individual and instead will give priority to the needs of family and community. They will become a person of *in* (C. *ren*), a Confucian term that is sometimes translated as "humanity" and other times as "benevolence." *In* means to empa-thize with people and things around you so that their best interests are as important to you as your own. To think and act in an *in* fash-ion is to act and think in the way human beings should act and think. In other words, it is the way to be fully human.

This, in brief, is the philosophical Confucianism that dominated the thinking and writing of the educated elite in the Chosŏn king-dom. The average Chosŏn kingdom Korean, however, continued to pray to the deities of the folk tradition and Buddhism for help in overcoming personal problems such as illness, crop failure, or a de-manding mother-in-law. They didn't have the time to study the Con-fucian Classics or sit in meditation quieting their selfish emotions.

The impact on the general population of the rise of Neo-Confu-cianism to official hegemony in Chosŏn Korea is seen primarily in language and in family structure. Confucian ethical terminology has come to dominate popular portrayals of proper and improper behav-ior. In addition, families in Korean villages began to conform more closely to the Confucian patriarchal model of what a family should look like, and those families came more and more to honor their im-mediate ancestors with Confucian rituals.

Neo-Confucianism was less effective in its attacks on folk religion and popular Buddhism. Neo-Confucianism argued that the world was controlled by impersonal forces, which made prayers for inter-vention by supernatural personalities a waste of time and resources. In the Neo-Confucian vision of the universe, untoward events such as floods and epidemics occurred when we acted out of narrow self-interest and therefore against the natural flow of events. If we put in-dividual concerns aside and instead cooperate with family members, neighbors, and nature itself, then the universe will function harmo-niously and we won't encounter such unpleasant surprises; or, if we did, our harmonious society would be able to cope with them.

Neo-Confucianism did not totally deny the existence of supernatural entities, but the Neo-Confucian Chosŏn government tried to control interaction with those entities by placing both monks and shamans under strict government control. The Chosŏn government's Neo-Confucian argument was that unregulated interaction with supernatural personalities would interfere with the natural patterns of interaction within nature and between nature and humanity and therefore should be minimized. The masses did not listen, however, and continued to visit temples and patronize shamans to seek supernatural assistance.

Because Neo-Confucianism was so closely associated with the ruling elite of the Chosŏn kingdom, when that kingdom fell to Japanese imperialism in 1910, Neo-Confucianism lost its hegemony as well. About the only place in contemporary Korea you can hear serious discussions of *li* and *ki* as the main formative forces in the cosmos are philosophy departments on university campuses. Even there, philosophies imported from the West have more adherents than Neo-Confucianism currently does.

The low profile of Neo-Confucianism in contemporary Korea does not mean that Confucianism no longer plays a significant role in Korean spirituality. On the contrary. Confucian ethics continue to provide the parameters for Korean concepts of the proper roles men and women should play in their families and communities. Koreans continue to value filial piety, loyalty, and sincerity. For more than half the South Korean population, modernized Confucian rituals serve as the primary way to show respect for deceased parents and grandparents. Both governments and large corporations borrow the ethical terminology of Confucianism to encourage their citizens and employees to subordinate personal desires to the proclaimed needs of the nation and the company, respectively.

Korea remains a Confucian society in many respects. Korean spirituality continues to be shaped by a greater concern for transcending the limitations of existence as an individual than for transcending the limitations of existence in a material world. Moreover, there is a collective orientation to Korean spirituality, an orientation that favors the family and the community over the individual. Confucian ethics reinforces the focus on overcoming individualism and individuality already present in folk religion and Buddhism, and it ensures that distrust of the unbridled pursuit of personal benefit remains a defining characteristic of Korean spirituality, even though Confucianism, Buddhism, and the folk religion are now being challenged by new forms of spirituality on the peninsula.

Daoism

One of the more individualist challenges to traditional spirituality is old rather than new, but the challenge was not a strong one. Daoism was one of the Three Teachings of China and as such arrived on the peninsula not long after Buddhism and Confucianism. Despite its early arrival, it never established an institutional presence on the same scale as its siblings. There were no halls for the study of Daoism, though there were plenty of Confucian and Neo-Confucian academies established over the centuries. Nor were there Daoist temples in Korea's mountains, though Buddhist temples were scattered all over the peninsula. The only Daoist temples in Korea were official temples located in the capital for the use of the government. Nevertheless, Daoism, broadly defined, contributed identifiable strands to the fabric that is Korean spirituality.

The term "Daoism" is used for an even wider variety of activities than Buddhists and Confucians engage in. The Daoist label is applied to liturgical Daoism (of the sort seen in Daoist temples), to the philosophy of Laozi and Zhuangzi, to the physiological transformation techniques of internal alchemists, and to calculations of longevity based on moral arithmetic. All were present on the peninsula at one time or another, and internal alchemy still exerts influence today, but none of those forms of Daoism gained the widespread popularity and independence that Buddhism, Confucianism, and even folk religion have enjoyed.

Daoist philosophy has had little impact on Korean philosophizing or Korean notions of transcendence. Koreans were not particularly persuaded that "nonaction"—the Daoist term for passive noninterference in the natural flow of events—was better than deliberate action in harmony with the natural flow of events, as recommended by Neo-Confucianism. Nor did those Koreans who could afford an upper-class education in classical Chinese (in other words, those who enjoyed a position at the top of a hereditary social pyramid) find much to like about the Daoist argument that social rankings were arbitrary and without merit. Liturgical Daoism had intermittent periods of support from Korean governments. In the seventh century, the government of Koguryŏ erected two Daoist temples and staffed them with priests from China in the hope that Daoist gods would prove more powerful than Buddhist deities and allow Koguryŏ to defeat the other two kingdoms vying with it for domination of the peninsula. When the Buddhist Silla kingdom defeated Koguryŏ, liturgical Daoism fell out of favor, not to return again until the rise of the Koryŏ kingdom in the tenth century. Koryŏ, which considered itself an heir to both Silla and Koguryŏ, hedged its bets, supporting a few Daoist temples around its capital in addition to a nationwide network of Buddhist temples. One of those Koryŏ Daoist temples survived the transition to the Chosŏn kingdom in 1392, but a lack of interest from Neo-Confucian officials meant that when the Office for Enshrining Deities was destroyed in the Japanese invasions of the 1590s, it was never rebuilt. All that remains of temple Daoism in contemporary Korea is a park near where that last temple stood. (Few in Korea today are aware that the name of that park, "The Park of the Three Pure Ones," is a reference to Daoist deities.) There were never any Daoist temples in outlying areas to preserve a Korean tradition of liturgical Daoism once official support was withdrawn.

Ironically, after the disappearance of the last Daoist temple, Buddhist temples began publishing and distributing Daoist works. Particularly popular were the *Classic of the Jade Pivot* and the *Classic of the Big Dipper*. Both works focused on celestial deities believed to play an important role in determining human fate and fortune. By the nineteenth century, those books were supplemented by moral arithmetic books, which allowed those concerned about how much longer they would be alive to calculate the remaining length of their allotted life span. Moral arithmetic books listed how many days certain good deeds would add to a life and how many days specified evil deeds would subtract. Moral arithmetic fell out of favor in the twentieth century, but Korean translations of the *Classic of the Jade Pivot* and the *Classic of the Big Dipper* can still occasionally be found on the shelves of Korean bookstores.

The form of Daoism most visible in Korea today, however, is internal alchemy, with its techniques of physiological transformation. Internal alchemy became so popular in South Korea during the last two decades of the twentieth century that many Koreans believe it is an integral part of traditional Korean culture that originated in ancient Korea rather than in China. However, the first evidence we can find for internal alchemy on the Korean peninsula, in the middle of the Chosŏn period, makes clear that the interest in internal alchemy was first sparked by books on that subject imported from China.

Internal alchemy is the name outsiders give to certain physical exercises, breathing techniques, and modes of meditation that are believed to enhance health and longevity by expelling bad *ki* from a practitioner's body and increasing the amount of good *ki*. Internal alchemy *ki* is the same *ki* Neo-Confucians talk about, but in internal alchemy it has a more restricted meaning. When internal alchemy practitioners talk about *ki,* they are talking about the energy of the universe serving as the vital force within our bodies that keeps us alive and healthy.

Internal alchemy was not limited to Daoists. Some of the leading Neo-Confucian scholars in the middle of the Chosŏn era used techniques of internal alchemy to fulfill the Confucian injunction to keep their bodies healthy enough to serve their parents properly. When internal alchemy was revived in the 1970s and 1980s, it adopted a more individualist tone. Practitioners are told now that through proper breathing techniques and physical exercises, accompanied by appropriate meditation, they will benefit personally from better health and vitality. Moreover, they are told that the specific techniques they are using were passed down in secret over several centuries from one mountain hermit to another. These mountain hermits, called "immortals," represent a rejection of the communitarian orientation of mainstream Korean spirituality, because they pursued longevity on their own and only shared the knowledge they gained with a select group of disciples.

Consequently, internal alchemy has been a minor thread in the fabric of Korean spirituality. Most Koreans continue to try to rise above the problems of this world by joining forces with supernatural beings or merging with invisible unifying forces in order to transcend the limitations of existence as an individual. The internal alchemy approach, which emphasizes overcoming the limitations of the individual physical body by augmenting an individual's allotment of *ki,* goes against the grain of traditional spirituality on the peninsula. Nevertheless, perhaps because urbanization is eroding the traditional group orientation of Koreans and stimulating individualism, such new internal alchemy organizations as Dahn World (discussed in chapter 5) are attracting thousands of practitioners in the cities and towns of Korea today.

CHAPTER 4

Korean Christianity

For most of their long history, Koreans looking for solutions to the types of problems religions and philosophies typically promise to solve could only look to folk religion, Buddhism, Confucianism, and sometimes Daoism for help. If they wanted to minimize or eliminate misfortune, such as ill health, economic setbacks, or poor interpersonal relations, they would ask shamans, monks, or scholars for help. However, they often found that they were unable to consistently do what those religious professionals told them to do, even though the Korean spiritual tradition told them they possessed the ability to overcome the limitations that were normally a part of human existence. Korean spirituality was caught in a dilemma, unwilling to deny the assumption of human perfectibility at the same time it was unable to ignore the reality of human frailty.

Near the end of the eighteenth century, Christianity entered the peninsula and gave Koreans new options for addressing old problems. Christianity and the new religions that followed it supplied new answers to such traditional problems as the presence of evil in the world and our inability to overcome it. These religions also provided new ways of conceiving and interacting with supernatural forces, new techniques for transcending the limitations of existence as an individual, and new approaches for resolving the contradiction between the presumption of human perfectibility and the reality of human moral weakness.

The old religions and philosophies did not disappear, of course. Though they were changed by their encounters with Christianity and other new religions, they continue to be the spirituality of choice for large numbers of Koreans. However, Koreans now have a much wider range of ways of addressing spiritual issues. Korea is now a veritable department store of spirituality that presents spiritual choices radically different from those available in the past.

For example, monotheism is now a visible religious option in Korea. None of the traditional religions were monotheistic; folk religion, popular Buddhism, and religious Daoism are clearly polytheistic, and philosophical Buddhism and Neo-Confucianism are nontheistic. However, Christianity introduced Koreans to the notion of a jealous God, a God who demanded that the righteous worship him and him alone and warned of dire consequences if they paid ritual homage to rival supernatural beings.

Faith-Based Communities

Along with devotion to one God and one God only, Christianity introduced a new meaning for the Sino-Korean character used for the traditional Confucian virtue of *shin*. In a pre-Christian context, *shin* usually means "trust" or "trustworthy." You could say that you trusted *(shin)* your friends, or you could say that your friends were trustworthy *(shin)*. However, you would not use the word *"shin"* in talking about the truth or falsity of religious doctrines or claims about the existence or nonexistence of a supernatural entity. *Shin* was used more in speaking of virtue than in asserting matters of fact. When you said you had *shin* in someone, you were talking about their personal qualities, not about whether you thought they existed or not. Before the arrival of Christianity, Koreans did not write that they believed *(shin)* in the existence of Buddha, Confucius, or God. Nor did they write that they believed *(shin)* in the teachings of Buddhism, Confucius, or shamans.

That changed when Christians appeared in Korea and began using the character *"shin"* for their faith, their unshakable conviction that God existed and that the Bible was his revealed truth. As Christians used the term, *shin* took on a whole new significance: it implied cognitive certainty more than it implied trustworthiness. Along with this shift in the meaning of *shin* from "trustworthy" to "faith" came another significant shift: Christians introduced the notion that your faith, your beliefs, determined which religious activities you could and could not engage in.

Korean Christians today proudly label their church congregations "faith-based communities." Before their encounter with Christianity, however, Koreans never would have conceived of such a term. If they had tried to find an analogous term to describe their traditional forms of spirituality, they would have said they participated in "ritual-based" communities. People could bring different beliefs about the nature of the gods or the efficacy of certain spiritual practices to a community ritual. Differences in beliefs were irrelevant as long as everyone performed their assigned roles in such rituals. For example, many peasants in traditional Korea believed that the spirits of the ancestors were actually present at ancestor memorial services. Confucian philosophers were more skeptical, but those scholars reasoned that the presence or absence of ancestral spirits was less important than whether participants in the ritual were sincere in their displays of reverence for their parents and grandparents, and whether participation in such rituals stimulated feelings of gratitude among the living toward the departed. In other words, what the participants in a ritual did and felt was more important than what they believed.

Such privileging of performance and emotion over belief was challenged by Korea's first Christians, who refused to participate in traditional ancestor memorial services. They argued that bowing before tablets representing the ancestors was a form of idolatry, because it implied that the ancestors were actually present in those tablets. In the ritual-based worldview of traditional Korean religion, such an objection to ancestor memorial services missed the point. Bowing before the tablet was not making a statement about whether the spirits of the ancestors were present in those tablets. It was not a physical expression of faith in the actual presence of the ancestors. Rather, bowing was a way for the descendants to show that they still loved and respected those who had brought them into this world. Moreover, participation in an ancestor memorial service reinforced family solidarity.

The Christian privileging of faith led to a greater emphasis on doctrine and orthodoxy than Koreans had seen previously. If you believe in one God, and you believe that one God has told you in writing what to believe, then it becomes essential that you believe what God has told you and reject anything that contradicts God's revelations.

That was a novel idea to Koreans in the eighteenth century. Before Christianity came to Korea, Koreans were not particularly concerned about creeds. Nontheistic Buddhists coexisted happily with polytheistic Buddhists, and shamans who did not agree about the powers, the characteristics, or even the names of their various gods could still work together and respect one another. Neo-Confucians probably came closer than any other spiritual community to condemning as heretics those who disagreed with them. However, a close examination of Neo-Confucian disputes reveals that they were much more concerned with different interpretations of the rules for performing rituals than with differences in their philosophical stances.

Christians were different, and the difference is manifest in the importance Christians place on the Bible. There was nothing comparable to the Hebrew Scriptures or the New Testament in Buddhism, Confucianism, or the folk religion. None of those traditions had a single compact volume that defined their core beliefs. Instead, there were many different Buddhist sutras, Confucian Classics, and shamanic oral traditions that both supplemented and contradicted other works in the same tradition. For example, a monk fond of the sutras that promised rebirth in Amitabha's paradise might share a monastery with a monk who focused on a sutra that explained how we could overcome the ignorance that misled us into thinking we are separate and distinct individuals. Neither monk would feel compelled to condemn the other as a heretic. Neo-Confucians were somewhat more concerned about preserving orthodoxy; for example, they would criticize a fellow Neo-Confucian scholar who believed that *li* could best be found by looking within our own mind rather than by investigating things. However, such criticism would not normally rise to the level of persecution or expulsion from the Neo-Confucian community unless that difference in textual interpretations led to differences in ritual performance. Orthopraxis (correct practice) was much more important to Neo-Confucians than orthodoxy (correct belief). What a person did was much more important than what a person believed.

In Christianity, however, emphasis on a more concise and clearly defined body of assertions that were to be believed (a creed), together with the greater certainty of belief that the term "faith" rather than "trust" implies, created an us-versus-them mentality. Faith in certain specific doctrines served as a boundary marker separating Christian believers from nonbelievers who did not agree that Jesus was the Son of God and had risen from the dead after being crucified by the Romans. A faith-defined spirituality thus creates more separate and distinct communities than a ritual-based spirituality does.

A faith-based spirituality also places more emphasis on the individual than ritual-based spirituality does. Ritual in traditional Korea was normally a group activity or at least an activity done on behalf of a group, such as one's family or village, rather than for one's own personal benefit. Of course, Christians have many communal rituals, but Christian faith primarily refers to what an individual believes rather than what a Christian community does. When someone says they believe in God, they are telling you what they as an individual believe; they are not making any claims about what their family and friends believe or do. A faith-based community is a community of people who share common beliefs but who nonetheless have each made an individual commitment to those articles of faith. Moreover, because one of those articles of faith for Christians is not only that a God exists but that people should enter into a positive personal relationship with that God, a faith-based spirituality such as Christianity places the individual's relationship with God above the individual's relationship with his or her family, neighbors, or government. This privileging of the individual relationship with God in Christianity has led to conflicts in modern Korean families. For example, an eldest son is normally expected to lead his siblings in ritual homage to their parents and grandparents. If that man's family is not a Christian family, they probably will express their homage with Confucian ritual. However, a Christian wife of a non-Christian eldest son often refuses to help with the preparation for such a ritual, because she does not want to encourage or participate in what she considers to be sinful idolatry. In such a situation, a non-Christian husband would want his wife to put her personal beliefs aside in the interest of family harmony. The wife, in turn, would insist that obedience to God's will is more important than what her in-laws think. The husband thinks the ritual is more important than personal beliefs, but his wife thinks her beliefs should determine what she should and should not do.

Even though religious communities that emphasize individual faith claim a substantial minority of today's Korean population as members, much of Korean spirituality retains the traditional focus on rituals associated with Confucianism and folk religion. A little more than two centuries ago, when Catholicism introduced Koreans to the concept of like-minded individuals joining together into faith-based communities defined along doctrinal lines, that challenge to traditional Korean spirituality encountered strong and sometimes violent resistance. During the first century and a half of Christian proselytizing on the Korean peninsula, only a small minority of Koreans accepted the more individualistic Christian approach to spirituality. Christianity and other faith-based religious bodies did not have much success in gaining recognition as mainstream organizations until the second half of the twentieth century, when industrialization and urbanization dissolved the traditional close-knit village societies in which the majority of Koreans used to live and drew them into cities that weakened family ties and stimulated individualism.

One product of the greater individuality that modernization allows is religious freedom: the freedom for an individual to profess religious beliefs or engage in spiritual practices without government interference. Before the second half of the twentieth century, Koreans did not enjoy freedom from government interference in their spiritual lives. The first converts to Catholicism in the late eighteenth century and to the new religion of Tonghak in the nineteenth century were persecuted by the Chosŏn dynasty for performing religious rituals forbidden by the state, and thousands of believers were killed. In the first half of the twentieth century, Japanese colonial authorities, who had seized control of Korea from the Chosŏn dynasty in 1910, jailed Christian leaders for refusing to honor the Japanese emperor with Shinto ritual. They also persecuted leaders of new religions for preaching belief in a "heavenly emperor" more powerful than the emperor of Japan.

Such attempts at government control of religious activity were not new to Korea. The Chosŏn dynasty, while still in its infancy in the fifteenth century, placed strict limits on the number of Buddhist monks and temples allowed in Korea, and it barred monks from even entering the capital city of Seoul. The Chosŏn dynasty also placed restrictions on shamans, telling them when they could and could not perform their rituals. Even Confucianism, though it was officially endorsed by the state, was not allowed complete freedom. The government placed limits on how many Confucian academies scholars could establish and on which Confucian sages they could enshrine in those academies. Such "religious freedom" as there was in premodern Korea existed only due to governmental inattention or to the government's inability to regulate every aspect of life on the peninsula. Government control of spirituality was still the norm when faith-based Christianity entered Korea and clashed with the ritual-centered Confucian state. The result was the first violent religious persecution in Korean history.

Roman Catholicism in Korea

When Christianity first entered Korea, the challenge it posed to traditional forms of spirituality was not well received. Many of Christianity's ideas were rejected and harshly criticized by the Neo-Confucian elite of the Chosŏn kingdom. However, there were a few conversions to Catholicism, and those early Catholics were not immediately subject to persecution. But when they began letting their new Christian beliefs influence their ritual behavior—in other words, when they formed a faith-based community—the Confucian state began to use force against them.

Ironically, Korea's first Catholics adopted Catholic teachings and rituals in order to become better Confucians. Though Catholic missionary publications written in classical Chinese had been circulating on the peninsula since early in the seventeenth century, it was not until the last quarter of the eighteenth century that some Koreans began taking those books seriously as guides to spirituality. In 1784 a young Confucian scholar named Yi Sŭnghun (1756–1801) returned from Beijing, where he had accompanied his father on a diplomatic mission, and announced to his friends that he had been baptized a Catholic by a French priest who lived in the Chinese capital. At that time there were no Catholic missionaries in Korea, so Peter Yi, as he now began calling himself, began preaching the new faith on his own. Yi quickly converted some of his relatives and Confucian scholar friends. Yi's friends and relatives were receptive to his proselytizing because he and they belonged to a wing of Korean Neo-Confucianism that was particularly sensitive to human moral frailty. The adherents to this strain of Neo-Confucianism had grown increasingly frustrated with their inability to reach the goal of sagehood that Confucianism told them was within their grasp. Catholic teachings attracted them with a new explanation for human moral frailty and the promise of a way to overcome it. That explanation lay in the Christian doctrine of original sin. Catholic publications taught that because Adam and Eve, the first human beings, disobeyed a direct command from God, their descendants (the entire human race) have been born with a propensity to selfishness. However, God is willing to help us overcome our innate selfish tendencies. By throwing ourselves on his mercy and availing ourselves of his divine assistance, we will be able to become the sages we all want to be. Catholicism thus promised a way to resolve the frustrating contradiction between the fact of human moral frailty and the assumption of human perfectibility by dropping the assumption that human perfectibility could be reached through human efforts alone.

A second reason that a small group of Confucian scholars found Catholicism appealing was their dissatisfaction with the impersonal foundation Neo-Confucianism provided for the Confucian ethics of interpersonal relations. Neo-Confucianism grounded human ethical obligations in *li,* the Neo-Confucian term for the unifying pattern of appropriate interactions that constitutes reality. However, *li* was not a god and had no will of its own. As one of Yi Sŭnghun's brothers-in-law, the famous philosopher Tasan Chŏng Yagyong (1762–1836), pointed out, *li* could not look at us with disapproving eyes to make us feel ashamed of our misdeeds. Therefore, *li* lacked the power to motivate us to eliminate selfish thoughts and actions. God, on the other hand, could see into our hearts and observe our every action. Such constant surveillance was a powerful incentive to virtuous thought and behavior.

In addition to a new explanation for human moral frailty and a new incentive to ethical thought and behavior, Catholicism offered new techniques for achieving sagehood. The Catholic missionary publications Koreans read in the seventeenth and eighteenth centuries told them, first of all, that there was only one true God in the world, and only those who declared their belief in that God and worshipped him would receive the help they needed to overcome the legacy of original sin and become virtuous. Those books told them that God channeled his assistance through certain rituals called "sacraments." Those sacraments were available only to those who had joined the faith-based community called the Roman Catholic Church. Moreover, some of these sacraments, which were essential to salvation, were only available through the mediation of a priest, a ritual specialist who had been certified as a channel for divine assistance by Catholic authorities.

Their search for a way to live in accordance with the rigorous demands of Confucian ethics led a number of young Koreans to conclude that ritual should be linked much more closely to correct belief, to "faith," than had been traditional in Korea. In the 1780s, those Koreans joined the Roman Catholic Church, a religious organization unlike any Korea had seen before. Not only did Catholicism welcome laypeople into full identification with that organization, allowing them to wear a religious label; it also required that they refrain from participation in non-Catholic ritual expressions of spirituality. Moreover, Catholicism had its own moral code, which it presented as the commands of God and which therefore overrode any commands from secular authorities such as a king or his officials.

In trying to become better Confucians, Korea's first Catholics ended up adopting new moral principles that did not conform to the moral principles the Chosŏn government expected all Koreans to adhere to. Male members of the Confucian scholarly elite in the Chosŏn kingdom were required to perform Confucian mourning rituals when their parents died. Catholics, however, were forbidden to perform or participate in such rituals. The pope in Rome had ruled early in the eighteenth century that such rituals were a form of ancestor worship, and those who performed them were guilty of idolatry, a sin that would bar them from the Catholic goal of eternal life with God in heaven. The papal ruling, which Korean Catholics did not learn of until a few years after they had already decided to join the Catholic Church, undercut attempts by Matteo Ricci (1552–1610) and other early Jesuit missionaries to China to present Catholicism as complementary to Confucianism rather than in conflict with it.

Once Korean Catholics learned of that decree in a 1790 letter from the bishop of Beijing, they realized that, rather than complementing Confucianism, Catholicism now claimed to supersede it by imposing new moral demands that placed sainthood (individual devotion to God) above sagehood (subordination of individual desire to the greater good of one's community). They were informed that they had to choose between Confucianism and Catholicism when it came to rituals such as the ancestor memorial service. When the mother of one of those new Korean Catholics died in 1791, her son obeyed the papal instructions and held an irregular funeral service for his mother, eliminating the ancestral tablet that had offended the pope. His deviation from Confucian tradition brought the wrath of his government down on him. Paul Yun Chich'ung (Paul was his baptismal name) was executed on December 8, 1791, becoming the first of thousands of Catholics to be martyred for their religious beliefs over the next century.

The immediate cause of Yun's execution was his scandalous alteration of the prescribed mourning ritual. However, a more serious offense, and the reason so many of his fellow Catholics suffered the same fate, was his challenge to the state's absolute authority over ritual. Before the modern era, Korean governments tolerated only those religious rituals that were held on their terms. The government prescribed which spirits could and should be worshipped, as well as when, how, and by whom. Any challenge to that ritual hegemony was seen as a challenge to the state itself and was met with the full power of the state's enforcement apparatus. Buddhists, shamans, and Confucian scholars usually did not find themselves in such a position, because they tended not to place a high priority on an individual's relationship with God. They were usually willing to put the demands of their community, including their government, before any individual expression of private belief. Catholics, however, believed that their relationship with God was more important than their relationship with their government. This departure from traditional Korean spirituality made the bloody conflict between the Chosŏn kingdom and the small Catholic community unavoidable.

The execution of Paul Yun in 1791 was only the beginning. A major persecution broke out in 1801 and took the lives of hundreds of

Korean Catholics, as well as the life of a Chinese priest who had been sent from Beijing in 1794 to minister to them. There were more widespread persecutions in 1839, 1846, and 1866–1869. Even the French priests who had been smuggled onto the peninsula after 1836 to nurture the infant Korean Catholic Church were tortured and executed. So many Koreans gave their lives for their imported faith that Korea now is dotted with signs marking sacred sites where Catholics were martyred in the eighteenth and nineteenth centuries. In addition, 103 members of the Korean Catholic community have received the highest honor their church can bestow: ninety-three Koreans and ten of the French priests who ministered to them have been officially certified by the Vatican as saints.

Not all the members of Korea's beleaguered Catholic community were captured by the Chosŏn kingdom's police. Thousands escaped into remote mountain valleys where they could hide from the government while they grew tobacco or made the earthenware pots in which Korean housewives stored food before the advent of refrigerators. Their main contacts with non-Catholic Koreans came from the infrequent trips they made out of their Catholic villages down to rural market towns to sell their goods. Otherwise, they tried to ignore the larger world around them. Fear of government persecution led them to create even higher walls around their faith-based community than they would have built otherwise. Even after official persecution ended in the 1880s, Korea's Catholics continued for several more decades to minimize contact with non-Catholics, marrying among themselves and living in villages populated by those who shared their faith.

It took Catholicism almost a century to overcome the effects of a century of persecution. Decades spent hiding from the outside world reinforced an already existing Catholic tendency to separate the spiritual realm from the material realm and to place more emphasis on the former. Until the second half of the twentieth century, Korean Catholics paid scant attention to Korea's need for modern institutions addressing such secular concerns as health and education. Consequently, Korean Catholics did not directly contribute much to the early stages of Korea's march to modernization, which began at the end of the nineteenth century.

The Catholic Church did not begin to attract substantial numbers of Koreans with a modern education and outlook until the second half of the twentieth century. In the aftermath of the Korean War, Korean Catholic priests began to greatly outnumber foreign missionary priests for the first time, giving the Korean Catholicism a more familiar face than it had had when it was run by Western bishops and priests. In addition, Korean Catholics began to imitate Protestants and open modern schools (including universities) and hospitals, giving Catholicism a more modern image. The result was a transformation of Korean Catholicism over the last four decades of the twentieth century into a well-educated and urban church, one that now claims the allegiance of more than five million Koreans.

Because of the new threads Catholicism introduced into the fabric that constitutes Korea's religious culture, spirituality in Korea today is more diverse than it was three centuries ago. First of all, Catholicism offered a new solution to the contradiction between the assumption that all human beings are born good and the reality that few of them are consistently good. Catholics placed more emphasis on the latter assertion at the expense of the former. This shift in the way this problem was traditionally conceived has forced even non-Christian Koreans to take human moral frailty more seriously.

Second, Catholicism made individual salvation the focus of religious effort, rather than subordinating individual benefit to what was best overall for a family, a village, or a country. Along with adding a more individualistic element to Korean spirituality, Catholicism introduced the notion of faith-based communities that were independent of the government as well as separate and distinct from other social organizations. The addition of this new concept of religion to Korean thinking about spirituality eventually helped lead to government neutrality in the religious marketplace, which gave South Koreans the religious freedom they enjoy today.

Third, because Catholicism was a faith-based religion, it introduced to Koreans the notion that a religion should have a succinct body of doctrine as its core. Before Catholics began distributing booklets explaining the basic tenets of their faith, Koreans had never seen a catechism. Nor had Koreans expected anyone, even religious professionals or Confucian scholars, to place as much weight on a single book as Christians placed on the Bible. The Bible was unlike any religious or philosophical text Koreans had seen before. It was much smaller than the multivolume collections, totaling thousands of pages, that Buddhists, Confucians, and Daoists drew on. In addition, Christians had much more confidence in what was written in the Bible than Koreans traditionally had in any single text. The strong faith Christians had in the Bible and the clarity it gave their doctrinal claims provided them with a proselytizing power that alarmed those who feared the Christian challenge would undermine traditional beliefs and practices. By the second half of the nineteenth century, non-Christians had begun to respond by producing their own "Bibles," one-volume compilations of their own sacred writings and doctrinal claims.

Possibly the most dramatic legacy of Catholicism in Korea is that it changed the way Koreans conceive of supernatural beings. Polytheism is still alive and well in contemporary Korea, but monotheism—or at least monodevotion to one spiritual force—is gaining ground. In fact, monotheism has become so respectable that in recent years many non-Christian scholars have begun claiming that Koreans were originally monotheists, before their indigenous spirituality was altered by its encounter with the Three Teachings from China.

Protestant Christianity

These alterations to Korean spirituality paved the way for the advances Protestant missionaries began making soon after their arrival in Korea in the 1880s. The first Protestant missionary, Horace Allen (1858–1932), arrived in Korea in 1884, at a time when Korean Catholics still feared persecution. However, he and the other Protestant missionaries who quickly followed him managed to establish a secure presence on Korean soil by offering their educational and medical skills to a government that was just beginning to awaken to the need for modern technology and institutions. Allen, a Presbyterian from the United States, opened Korea's first hospital for Western medicine in 1885 in the capital city of Seoul. The next year, U.S. Methodist missionaries opened two modern schools in Seoul. (One of those schools, the first school in Korea to provide formal education for women, later grew into Ewha Womans University, one of the largest all-female universities in the world today and regarded as one of the best universities in Korea.)

The Protestant missionaries also benefited from the fact that, within a few years after they arrived, a series of treaties with Western countries forced the Korean government to allow proselytizing by foreign missionaries and even to let Koreans adopt the religions those foreigners preached. At first, despite rapid growth in numerical terms, Protestant churches were unable to enroll more than a very small percentage of the overall Korean population. At the turn of the twentieth century, there were less than twenty thousand Protestant Christians on the entire Korean peninsula, out of a population of at least eleven million, making the Protestant community half the size of the Catholic community and outnumbered even by Tonghak, an outlawed new religion discussed in the next chapter.

That began to change in 1907. A series of revival meetings across the peninsula that year stimulated a rapid growth in membership in Protestant churches. By 1910 (the year the Japanese absorbed Korea into their colonial empire), there were more than one hundred forty thousand Protestants (mostly Presbyterians and Methodists), almost twice as many members as the Catholic community and also larger than the Tonghak community, even though Tonghak had by now been transformed into the legal Religion of the Heavenly Way. By the 1930s, Protestants were the single largest religious community in Korea, outnumbering even self-identified Buddhists by a sizable margin. How did this happen? How did a relative latecomer to the religious scene in Korea manage to gain so many believers so quickly that it came to dominate the religious landscape? Support from relatively wealthy foreign mission societies, which gave Protestant proselytizers a substantial financial advantage over their competitors, is one reason. Even Roman Catholic missionaries, though they received funds from France and other Catholic nations, did not receive the same level of support that the United States and the British Commonwealth provided Protestant missionaries. For example, in the 1920s, one foreign Catholic priest complained that Protestant missionaries typically had a budget about sixty times larger than the budget available to the average Catholic priest in Korea. Funds from abroad paid for both missionaries and the training of native clergy.

The Union Theological Seminary was established in Korea in 1901 to train Korean preachers and pastors. By 1916, there were thirty-eight Protestant pastors in Korea for every Catholic priest. There were also a lot more Protestant churches than Catholic ones.

With more salespeople and more retail outlets, it is not surprising that Protestants outsold their competition in the religious marketplace. But the scale of their operation was not the only advantage Protestants had. Their theology and the way they worshipped their God made Protestant Christianity an attractive alternative to traditional forms of spirituality as well as to the new Catholic and Heavenly Learning approaches.

Protestant pastors were the first Korean ritual specialists other than practitioners of the folk religion to use the language spoken in everyday life as the primary language of ritual. Catholics used Latin (until the 1960s); Confucians used classical Chinese, and Buddhists used a special form of classical Chinese as well as Sanskrit. Even the Religion of the Heavenly Way relied heavily on classical Chinese material. Protestants, however, translated their Bible into Korean, and they preached and prayed in Korean. Their preference for the vernacular made Protestant worship services easier for the average person to understand and less intimidating to those who might want to participate in them.

Moreover, Protestant worship services were participatory. Lay Buddhists watched monks perform their rituals, and villagers watched shamans dance and sing to persuade a god to do their bidding. Even Catholics knelt reverently in silence while their priests performed the miracle of the Eucharist with their backs to the congregation. But Protestants joined their pastors in joyful song, engaging in a form of congregational worship Koreans had never experienced before. The hymns they sang (in Korean translation) included the classics "What a Friend We Have in Jesus" and "Jesus Loves Me," fostering a more personal relationship with God than Korean spirituality had traditionally fostered. In addition, God was regularly referred to as "Father" in those hymns, and believers were encouraged to call themselves his children, adding the power of the language of family—with all its overtones of Confucian morality—to the theological assertions in those hymns.

Even the name Protestants used for God was chosen to make Koreans feel more comfortable calling his name. Korean Catholics referred to God as "Ch'ŏnju," an awkward Sino-Korean phrase meaning "Lord of Heaven" that had been coined by early Jesuit missionaries in China. As noted in the previous chapter, Buddhists had a number of names for the various buddhas and bodhisattvas, but none of them sounded like names Koreans would use in ordinary conversation among themselves. Shamans, like Buddhists, used a number of different names for the different spirits they interacted with, but none of the commonly used names referred to a supreme deity, and those that referred to particularly powerful deities, such as Okhwang Sangje (the Jade Emperor), had a distinctively foreign sound to them. Not long after they began preaching in Korea, however, Protestant missionaries decided they should avoid confusion with the gods of other religions by devising their own name for God. One name they came up with, "Hananim," meaning the One God, sounded Korean because it was composed of purely Korean elements. An alternative Protestant name for God, "Hanŭnim," a vernacular version of "Lord of Heaven," had occasionally been used by Koreans in times past, though never with the monotheistic connotations Protestant preachers gave it. Nevertheless, that term sounded so natural a name for God to Korean ears that many came to believe that it was a reflection of an ancient monotheistic tradition in Korea. These two natural-sounding names Protestants coined for God narrowed the distance between God and his believers, helping to draw Koreans into interaction with him through ritual and prayer.

In addition, the way Protestants worshipped their God gave them an advantage over other religious communities in attracting new members in Korea. Unlike Korean Catholic churches, the Religion of the Heavenly Way, Buddhism, and Confucianism, Protestant organizations organized large-scale revivals that resembled the rituals of charismatic shamans in emotional intensity, but on a much larger scale. Even the preaching and singing in ordinary Protestant Sunday worship services tended to be filled with a religious fervor not often seen in Korean rituals.

The intensity of Protestant revivals, preaching, and singing heightened the individual sensitivity to human moral frailty that had long been part of Korean spirituality. However, instead of abandoning the men and women in their pews to despair, Protestant congregations sang songs and read Bible passages assuring them that the friend they had in Jesus and their Father on high would rescue them from their sins and allow them to enjoy eternal life in heaven. The exhilaration those churchgoers felt when they finished this ride on an emotional roller-coaster often propelled them out the doors of their churches into the streets to entice others to join them. Korean Protestantism generated a proselytizing zeal Koreans had never seen before in lay members of religious communities.

Despite the enthusiasm with which Korea's first Protestants embraced and spread their faith, by the early 1940s they could claim no more than four hundred thousand fellow believers in a population now totaling almost twenty-four million. As noted earlier, Protestants were the largest religious community in Korea in the 1940s, but only around 3 percent of the peninsula's inhabitants claimed a specific religious affiliation. The majority of Koreans at that time remained immersed in village life, in which less self-conscious approaches to spirituality were the norm.

However, a series of events, starting with the Japanese departure from Korea in 1945 after World War II, began unraveling the bonds that held rural communities together. The return of millions of Koreans who had spent the war years in Japan or Manchuria eroded the insularity of rural society. The division of the peninsula in 1948 into a Communist north and a non-Communist south (under the leadership of Methodist president Syngman Rhee) drove hundreds of thousands of Koreans from the northern villages they had lived in for centuries, in a search for a less hostile political climate. The Korean War, which took place from 1950 to 1953, destroyed many villages and severely undermined the sense of community in those that survived. Then, in the 1960s, Korea began its rapid march to industrialization that drew peasants from their farms and out of their villages into factories and apartment complexes in rapidly expanding cities.

Bereft of the security that rural kinship and friendship networks had once provided, left to fend for themselves on bustling factory floors and crowded city streets, newly urbanized Koreans turned to religious groups for a new supportive network of friends and associates. The religious group most of them noticed first was Protestant Christianity, partially because its churches were more visible than the worship halls of other religious organizations. (Since the 1960s, approximately two-thirds of all houses of worship and one-third of all clergy in South Korea have been Protestant.) However, in addition to the ubiquity of churches, another reason Protestant churches often became the new community of choice for immigrants to Korea's cities was the enthusiastic evangelizing by the already converted, as well as the constant exposure to Christianity provided by Christian radio broadcasts and Christian schools and medical facilities. Soon Korea's Protestant churches began to add members at a rate that dramatically altered the religious landscape of South Korea.

In 1960 the various Protestant denominations in South Korea reported to their government that they had 623,072 members. One decade later, in 1970, they reported that their membership had grown 500 percent, to 3,192,621. That figure more than doubled again by 1980, with Protestant churches claiming to have 7,180,627 members that year. That figure may have been exaggerated somewhat, because the South Korean government found only 6,489,282 Protestants in its 1985 census. Nevertheless, it was clear that, even with the lower official figure, the Protestant community in South Korea had, sometime in the 1960s, embarked on a period of sustained, breathtaking growth. By 2005, according to the census that year, there were around 8.6 million Protestants in Korea, almost fourteen times more than there had been less than fifty years earlier.

Growth has brought with it growing pains, revealed in the fragmentation of the dominant Protestant denominations into many subdenominations. Ironically, such fragmentation might have increased the rate of growth, with competition among churches stimulating even more proselytizing activity. Koreans now brag that they have the world's largest Christian congregation (the Yoido Full Gospel Church claims seven hundred thousand members) as well as what may be the world's largest Presbyterian congregation (Youngnak Church, with more than sixty thousand members).

In a break with tradition, Korean Protestants are much more text- and doctrine-oriented than their non-Christian ancestors tended to be. In fact, most of Korea's Protestant preachers are fundamental-

Young Korean Christians enthusiastically proclaiming their faith in song.
Photo by Min Cheal Kim and Jeong Muk Oh from the Korean Academy
of Church History of the Korean Evangelical Holiness Church in Seoul.

ists, regularly affirming the inspired inerrancy of the Bible. Moreover, Korean evangelists often insist that those who do not accept
the Christian Gospel, as they define it, will be condemned to eternal
damnation, thus rejecting the doctrinal flexibility that was a mark of
traditional Korean spirituality. Though followers of other religious
traditions in Korea — even Roman Catholics — have no qualms about
visiting a Buddhist temple in the mountains to admire the scenery and the traditional art and architecture, devout Protestants stay
away, reluctant to give even the appearance of tolerating what they
believe are false teachings. Korea's Protestants place more emphasis
on correct faith than members of other faith-based communities in
modern Korea do, including Korea's Catholics. Catholics preach that
both faith and good works are necessary for salvation, but Korea's
Protestants tend to believe in justification through faith alone.

    Korean Protestants also set themselves apart from most of their
fellow Koreans, and reinforce their sense of constituting a separate
and distinct community, by following a much more rigid moral code

than is usually associated with Korean spirituality. For example, Korean Protestants are not supposed to use tobacco or alcohol, even though Korean men in general are among the heaviest smokers and drinkers in the world. Korean Protestants do sing, though many of them are suspicious of popular music that does not sing the praises of God or Jesus.

But their strict moral code does not mean that Korean Protestants are a dour group. Mainstream Korean Protestant churches display an exuberance that in North America is usually associated with Pentecostal churches. Protestant services in Korea are often filled with loud, fervent prayers and confessions of faith, and with enthusiastic and joyful singing and praise for the Lord. Perhaps remembering their ancestors' experiences with shamanic possession, Korean Christians often look for and expect concrete signs that they or their follow worshippers have been filled with the Holy Spirit. Speaking in tongues is not unusual in mainstream Korean churches. In addition, many Protestants, especially women believers, attend church not only on Sundays but on weekdays as well. Most churches provide weekday predawn services for those who wish to pray or worship before they begin the day's work. I vividly remember once walking down the street near my Seoul home at five a.m. on a weekday morning (jet lag had pushed me out of bed) when loud singing suddenly broke out from buildings all around me. Predawn church services had begun.

The sound of Christian hymns filling the streets of pre-dawn Seoul was an audible confirmation of the dramatic transformation Korean spirituality has undergone over the last century. Christianity, once invisible on the Korean peninsula, now claims the allegiance of almost one out of every three South Koreans. This surge in the size and numbers of Christian faith-based communities has stimulated an increase in non-Christian religiosity as well. As the number of Catholic and Protestant churches has grown, so has the number of shamans active in Korea's cities and the number of new Buddhist temples appearing both in cities and the countryside. Moreover, Koreans have begun to create their own indigenous organized religions. In the next chapter, we will look at some of these new Korean religions.

CHAPTER 5

The New Religions of Korea

Christianity introduced Korea to a new approach to spirituality that differed significantly from the traditional approach. For example, Korean Christians are more concerned about the specifics of what their religious community believes than their non-Christian ancestors were. This emphasis on doctrine and creed does not mean, of course, that Christians don't think rituals are important. Quite the contrary: rituals gain importance in Christian eyes as outward manifestations of faith.

Such linking of ritual with faith has two important implications. First of all, Christians will not take part in rituals incompatible with Christian faith. As monotheists, they refuse to engage in any behavior that implies worship of anyone or anything other than the Christian God. (We saw in the last chapter that the Catholic refusal to bow before the spirit tablets of departed loved ones was one reason Catholics were persecuted for almost a century.) Second, when faith and ritual are closely intertwined, as they are in Christianity, all those who believe in the same creed, clergy and laity alike, are usually expected to participate regularly in the rituals affirming their faith. The resulting faith-based community of believers, who meet regularly for rituals of worship and prayer and who refuse individually to participate in the rituals of any other religious community, erects walls of faith and practice that separate it from other religious communities. A common creed reinforced by communal rituals promotes a feeling of belonging to the group. The Christian fusion of faith and ritual leads to adoption of a specific and exclusive religion affiliation.

We saw in the introductory chapter that over the course of the twentieth century, more and more Koreans have begun adopting religious labels. Not every Korean who does so is Christian; Koreans who frequent temples are increasingly identifying as Buddhists. Christianity has also stimulated the emergence of many new religions. Those new religions resemble Christianity in the ways they define themselves and distinguish themselves from other religious communities. Like Christianity, Korea's new religions are faith-based communities, differentiated from other religions not so much by the rituals they perform and the moral codes they promote as by the unique gods they worship, the distinctive doctrines they teach, and the texts they—and they alone—hold sacred.

Eastern Learning (the Religion of the Heavenly Way)

Korea's first indigenous organized religion emerged in 1860, partially in response to the changes in Korean spirituality stimulated by the introduction of Catholicism to the peninsula. Ch'oe Cheu (1824–1864) founded this new religion, which he called "Eastern Learning" (Tonghak) to distinguish it from "Western Learning" (an early Korean name for Catholicism). He claimed that God appeared to him on April 5, 1860, and told him that he had been selected to save mankind. Conversing with supernatural beings was not unusual in Korea—shamans regularly talked to spirits in their rituals—but Ch'oe's experience was different. He claimed that he had talked with the one and only God, though he addressed that God under three different names. Sometimes he called God the "Lord of Heaven" (the name preferred by Catholics in China and Korea), sometimes he used the term "Sangje" (the Lord on High of ancient Confucian texts), and once in a while he called God "Hanullim," a Korean translation of "Lord of Heaven." Nevertheless, it is clear that Ch'oe was referring to only one God and did not subscribe to the polytheism that had dominated traditional Korean spirituality.

Abandoning polytheism was a risky step, made more dangerous by Ch'oe's use of the Catholic name for God. Ch'oe was arrested and hanged in 1864 for behaving more like a Catholic than like a traditional Korean by preaching what the state viewed as subversive doctrines that undermined its all-inclusive authority. When there are many gods and supernatural power is divided among them, the state can stand above them. When there is only one God in whom all supernatural power is concentrated, however, that God towers above the state and can invalidate the state's commands. The government

A statue of Ch'oe Cheu at the entrance to Yongdam Pavilion, where he received the revelation that inspired him to found the Tonghak religion. Author photo.

of Korea, accustomed to supreme authority even in religious matters, could not tolerate such a challenge.

If he had not preached monotheism, Ch'oe Cheu might have been able to escape the government's wrath. Most of what he taught his followers was not new. Most of his moral principles were Confucian, as was much of his vocabulary. His writings, which now constitute the opening section of the one-volume scripture his followers rely on today, are filled with traditional Confucian exhortations to cultivate the virtues of sincerity and reverence. When he advised his followers that they would be protected from disease if they drew a sacred talisman, took the piece of paper on which that talisman was written, burned it, mixed the ashes in water, and drank that water, he was engaging in the sort of behavior the government had long tolerated in shamans. In addition, he called his teachings "Eastern Learning" (Tonghak) to indicate that he was trying to defend the traditional values and beliefs of the East against the challenge of "Western Learning."

What made the government so hostile to Ch'oe and his Tonghak were the Catholic elements, such as the focus on one God, that he added to traditional Korean spirituality. Along with monotheism came another idea borrowed from Catholicism: the notion that belief in one God made Tonghak followers a group separate from the rest of society. Like Catholicism—but unlike Buddhism, Korean Daoism, and the folk religion—Tonghak had an initiation ritual that represented the lay believer's joining a community of faith. Tonghak practitioners also performed other rituals that were not authorized by the government and were therefore illegal.

Though Ch'oe was hanged only four years after his first revelations, his religion did not die with him. Instead, Tonghak joined Catholicism in the religious underground that had begun to challenge the foundations of traditional Korean spirituality. It remained a monotheistic religion, though Ch'oe's monotheistic message was modified by his successors to describe God less as a supernatural personality and more as an impersonal moral presence, much like the Neo-Confucian *li*, that fills the entire universe and dwells within every human heart.

By the early twentieth century, Tonghak leaders were preaching that God did not dwell in the skies above. Instead, God could be found in every man, woman, and child on the earth below, because a spark of the divine was present within everyone. For peasants and merchants who had been told for centuries by the Confucian ruling elite that those who worked with their hands were inferior to those who worked with their heads, and for women who had been told for even longer that their gender made them lesser human beings, the assertion that all human beings were worthy of respect must have been very attractive.

Tonghak teachings offered more than consolation to those of low social status. It also offered hope that the hierarchical structure of Korean society would soon be transformed into something more egalitarian. Ch'oe Cheu taught that it had been fifty thousand years since the universe came into existence. However, its time was coming to an end and a new era was dawning. How that Great Transformation would unfold—whether it would primarily consist of changes in the cosmos or changes in the human heart—was uncertain. What was clear, however, was that after the Great Transformation, life on earth would be much better. There would be no more injustice, poverty, or disease, and Korea and all of her people would be treated with the respect they deserved.

The promise of a Great Transformation might have been one of the inspirations for the largest peasant rebellion in Korean history. In 1894, rebels using the Tonghak name and organization rose up in armed protest against government corruption and the growing presence of Japanese and Westerners on Korean soil. When that rebellion was crushed, Tonghak was forced deeper underground. When it finally resurfaced as a legal organization ten years later, in 1905, it adopted a new name: Ch'ŏndogyo, the Religion of the Heavenly Way.

The Religion of the Heavenly Way survives today as a modern religion, with standardized doctrine and ritual, a centralized administrative structure based in an urban headquarters, and regular Sunday congregational worship services in churches that resemble the worship halls Protestant Christians began erecting in Korea at the end of the nineteenth century. The religion no longer attracts many active members. Though it claims to operate 281 worship halls and to have one million names on its membership rolls, in the 2005 census fewer than fifty thousand people checked "Ch'ŏndogyo" as their religious affiliation. Believers gather every Sunday morning to read the revered writings of Ch'oe Cheu and his two successors in a bound volume that resembles the Christian Bible, to sing hymns drawn largely from those writings, and to listen to sermons expounding on the lessons taught by the sacred texts.

The most important religious practice of the Religion of the Heavenly Way is the recitation of incantations, particularly a twenty-one-syllable incantation that Ch'oe Cheu taught his first disciples. It can be translated thus: "Ultimate Energy being all around me, I pray that I feel that Energy within me here and now. Recognizing that the Lord of Heaven is within me, I will be transformed. Constantly aware of that divine presence within, I will become attuned to all that is going on around me." In reciting that incantation, believers are praying that they will be filled with the animating energy of the cosmos so that they may feel God's presence within them and will therefore be moved to act in harmony with God's creation. Religion of the Heavenly Way leaders say that repeated recitation of that incantation heightens awareness of the presence of God within us and stimulates us to act in accordance with that awareness. Moreover, devout believers report that sometimes, when chanting that incantation, they can actually feel divine energy enter their bodies and can experience the ecstasy of being one with God and the cosmos. That religious experience is supposed to lead to more God-directed behavior. Because Ch'ŏndogyo is an indigenous Korean religion, it accepts the basic ethical vocabulary of Confucianism. It assumes that someone who maintains awareness of the presence of God within them will, in their thoughts and their actions, display sincerity, reverence, and faith.

Sincerity in Ch'ŏndogyo, as in Confucianism, means thinking and acting as a member of a larger community instead of selfishly pursuing personal self-interest. Reverence in both Ch'ŏndogyo and Confucianism refers to an attitude of respect for all the people we encounter as well as for the natural environment that surrounds and nurtures us and for the underlying cosmic network that provides the foundation for the harmonious interaction of everything and everyone in the universe. However, Ch'ŏndogyo defines the grounds for sincerity and reverence in terms orthodox Neo-Confucians would never use. Ch'ŏndogyo tells us to be sincere and respectful toward every human being we encounter because there is a spark of the divine within every human being.

Though Ch'ŏndogyo names its third cardinal virtue *"shin,"* a term Confucians also used, Ch'ŏndogyo uses that term to mean "faith," a usage rarely seen in Confucianism but prominent in the writings of Catholics, who were in Korea for more than half a century before Ch'ŏndogyo appeared. We have already seen that the character *"shin"* usually means "trust" or "trustworthy" when Confucians use that term. For example, Confucians mention trust between friends as one of the five most important virtues governing human relationships. However, *shin* means "belief that something is true" in Ch'ŏndogyo, just as it does in Christianity. In the case of Ch'ŏndogyo, *shin* means belief that God is not some supernatural personality in heaven above but a spiritual force that resides within us all. The Ch'ŏndogyo scriptures add that unless we truly believe that God lives within human beings, and that therefore we should accord every human being the same respect we should accord God, we will not be able to exemplify the four important Confucian virtues of benevolence, righteousness, propriety, and wisdom in our daily lives.

Ch'ŏndogyo also teaches that we can discipline ourselves to act with sincerity, reverence, and faith by "preserving our original pure mind and rectifying our psycho-physical endowment." The concept of "original pure mind" is similar to the concept of "human nature" that is so important in Neo-Confucian moral discourse. Both of these concepts represent innate goodness, the natural ability to perceive and respond to our social and natural environment without any distortions introduced by considerations of narrow personal self-interest. However, rather than following the Neo-Confucian example and identifying that innate goodness with *li,* the impersonal cosmic network of appropriate interactions, Ch'ŏndogyo identified our innate goodness with God.

In a further break with Neo-Confucian orthodoxy, Ch'ŏndogyo defined God more in terms of *ki* (in Neo-Confucianism, the matter-energy of which everything in the universe is composed) than of *li.* God, in Ch'ŏndogyo, is a name for the dynamic creative energy that sustains the universe and is responsible for the many harmonious transformations that produce objects and natural phenomena within that universe. When we rectify our psychophysical endowment, understood as that portion of *ki* that forms our bodies and our minds, we eliminate the distortions of selfishness that keep us from actualizing our innate power to contribute to the divine cosmic creative process and build a better, more harmonious world. How can we rectify our psychophysical endowment? Ch'ŏndogyo scriptures tell us that the best way to do that is to be filial toward our parents, deferential toward elders and our older siblings, and honest with our friends. In other words, if we act in accordance with the traditional Confucian ethical injunctions, we will develop the sort of moral character that Ch'ŏndogyo advises us to develop.

Ch'ŏndogyo, with its Confucian-influenced ethics grounded in a novel theology, reached its peak of popularity during the bleak years of Japanese colonial rule. It maintains a small membership in both North and South Korea, but it is no longer the largest new Korean religion. Instead, Ch'ŏndogyo is now overshadowed by many other new religions.

The Chŭngsan Family of Religions

Among the largest new Korean religions today are the religions focused on worship of Kang Chŭngsan (1871–1909) as the supreme deity. The Chŭngsan family of religions is neither Buddhist nor Confucian nor Christian; nor is it simply an organized form of Korea's folk religion. Nether is it a branch of Ch'ŏndogyo, though it views Ch'oe Cheu as a prophet who prepared the people of Korea for the arrival of God incarnate among them.

The Chŭngsan religions are distinguished from all other religions by the unique god they worship and the unique rituals they say their god has told them to perform. They teach that the supreme deity descended to earth at the end of the nineteenth century and took human form in Korea under the name of Kang Chŭngsan. Koreans who worship Kang Chŭngsan as God address him as "Sangjenim" (Honorable Lord on High) and believe that he descended from his heavenly throne to Korea in order to teach humanity the Rites of Cosmic Renewal. They believe that those rites will hasten the Great Transformation from the current age of discord and injustice to the coming age of cosmic harmony.

There are dozens of religious organizations dedicated to the worship of Sangjenim. The best known are Jeung San Do and Daesun Jinri-hoe (sometimes spelled Daesoonjinrihoe). Jeung San Do is the most active overseas, attracting followers not only in Korea but also in North America, Europe, Japan, Taiwan, and Australia with its eschatological predictions of a cosmic cataclysm that will be followed by a Great Transformation producing a terrestrial paradise for believers to enjoy. It claims to have around three hundred thousand members worldwide. In Korea itself, however, Jeung San Do is overshadowed by Daesun Jinri-hoe, which claims to have more than six million members (though fewer than thirty-five thousand gave a Chŭngsan religion as their religious affiliation in the 2005 census).

A worship hall in a Daesun Jinri-hoe shrine. Photo courtesy of the Academy of Daesoon Thought of Daejin University.

Daesun Jinri-hoe emphasizes the ethical teachings of Kang Chŭng-san more than his cosmological predictions. It is known in Korea for the schools and medical facilities it has built to implement Kang's call to better the lives of others by creating a world of mutual aid and cooperation to replace the current atmosphere of competition and conflict. Daesun Jinri-hoe draws much of its appeal from the traditional ethical terminology it uses. Like Ch'ŏndogyo, it draws on vocabulary rooted in Confucian tradition. However, Daesun Jinri-hoe, more than other major indigenous religions in Korea, recognizes that the Confucian ethics of patriarchy and a social hierarchy cause problems that need to be addressed and resolved. It proposes to address those problems with what may be called a post-Confucian ethics.

The Confucian component of Daesun Jinri-hoe ethical philosophy appears in what Daesun Jinri-hoe calls its "three cardinal points." Those cardinal points, which would be better understood as three primary virtues, are the familiar Confucian triad of sincerity, reverence, and trust. Those three terms retain in Daesun Jinri-hoe the meanings they had in Confucianism. Sincerity continues to refer to doing what you are supposed to do as a member of your family, community, and nation instead of pursuing your own narrow self-interest. Reverence continues to mean an attitude of respect for the social and natural world that surrounds you, an attitude that should inspire you to concentrate on your obligations in that world with utmost seriousness. And trust continues to mean trustworthiness, always acting in such a way that others can rely on you.

However, Daesun Jinri-hoe adds theistic connotations to those three Confucian virtues. In Daesun Jinri-hoe theology, trust refers not only to being trustworthy in your dealings with other human beings; it also means to trust the assertion that Kang Chŭngsan is Sangjenim, the Supreme Ruler Above, and to believe that the advice he offered humanity when he walked on Korean soil at the beginning of the twentieth century is advice all men and women should follow. In Daesun Jinri-hoe, reverence means not just reverence toward all things in general but also a reverent attitude toward Sangjenim, demonstrated by keeping him in your thoughts at all times and following his instructions to the letter when participating in Daesun Jinri-hoe rituals. Sincerity means not just doing what you are sup-

posed to do in your daily life but also performing rituals taught by
Sangjenim and following Sangjenim's ethical injunctions with complete confidence that those rituals are effective and those precepts are
appropriate.

In addition to these Confucian virtues, Daesun Jinri-hoe adds new
moral principles. Two core concepts in Daesun Jinri-hoe's message
are *haewon* and *sangsaeng*. *Haewon* means relieving the resentment
human beings past and present have felt because they were treated
unfairly. Particularly aggrieved are women and the poor, because, according to Daesun Jinri-hoe, Confucianism and other hierarchical,
patriarchal philosophies have forced them to subordinate their own
wants and needs to the desires of their overlords. To alleviate such resentment, members of Daesun Jinri-hoe are told to treat women and
the poor of today with respect and to conduct appropriate rituals to
relieve the resentment of the spirits of those mistreated in the past.

Daesun Jinri-hoe members are also told to live *sangsaeng* lives
—lives characterized by a spirit of mutual aid and cooperation rather
than by the spirit of competition and conflict that has dominated the
human community up to the present day. The term *"sangsaeng"* is
the opposite of the term *"sanggŭk,"* literally "mutual overcoming."
Sanggŭk refers to the traditional belief that the universe is filled with
conflict that constantly generates winners and losers, reflected in an
ever-changing hierarchy. *Sangsaeng* is the way to put an end to such
conflict and the inequality it produces. Together *haewon* and *sangsaeng* tell us to stop trying to gain personal benefit at the expense of
others and instead to put others' interests before our own. By doing
so, we will not only avoid creating new resentments; we will create
new relationships of love and trust that will erase the old feelings of
resentment and anger.

Daesun Jinri-hoe also offers more specific ethical guidelines for
its followers. There are no rules telling Daesun Jinri-hoe members
they can't smoke, drink, or eat meat, but they are told to act in accordance with traditional Confucian moral principles, such as being
filial to their parents and loyal to their country. They are also told to
respect their elders and maintain a spirit of harmonious cooperation
between spouses and a spirit of trust between friends. In addition,
they are told to always act in such a way as to put the best interests of

others first and to refrain from any words or actions that cause ill will or resentment in others. They should refrain from misleading others with false statements. Finally, they are told they should be brutally honest with themselves so they will recognize when they are acting more out of self-interest than out of sincerity and altruism.

Won Buddhism

Not all of Korea's new religions borrow as heavily from Confucianism as Ch'ŏndogyo and the Chŭngsan religions do. The largest new religion, Won Buddhism, is more Buddhist than Confucian in orientation, as its name proclaims. The 2005 census counted almost one hundred thirty thousand Won Buddhists in Korea. (Won Buddhists claim that they have more than 1.3 million people attending their more than four hundred fifty temples.) Won Buddhism was listed separately from mainstream Buddhism on the census form because Won Buddhists insist that theirs is a new religion. Won Buddhism calls itself a new religion because it teaches a new approach to Buddhism, a Buddhism for everyday life in the modern world, rather than the traditional Buddhism better suited for monks in isolated rural areas. It builds its worship halls on urban streets rather than on mountain slopes. Moreover, you will not find any statutes of buddhas or bodhisattvas in a Won Buddhist temple. Instead, you will see pews, a pulpit, and, on the wall in the front of the hall, a single circle to remind believers that everything in the universe has the same origin and shares the same basic nature.

Won Buddhism's departure from traditional Buddhism is revealed not only in the absence of statues in its temples but also in the composition of its clergy. Mainstream Buddhism is largely patriarchal, with nuns usually playing a supportive role to the leadership of monks. Won Buddhism, on the other hand, gives its nuns a very active role, both in its headquarters and in local temples. Though the national leaders of Won Buddhism are predominantly male, at the local level female clergy often wield as much authority as male clergy do. (One major difference between them remains, however. Male clergy normally are married; female clergy are celibate.)

However, we can still see some signs of traditional Confucian values in Won Buddhism's ethical teachings. Won Buddhism stands closer to the Confucian emphasis on selfless action to improve conditions in this world than to the philosophical Buddhist focus on detachment from this world, and it preaches an ethical orientation that is, in its own words, an extension of the Confucian virtue of filial piety. Won Buddhism teaches that, just as children should acknowledge the debt of gratitude they owe the parents who gave them life, so should all human beings acknowledge how much they owe the four forces that underlie their very existence as human beings. We should of course feel grateful to our parents, who brought us into this world, but we should also feel grateful to heaven and earth for providing the air we breathe and the soil on which we stand. We should also recognize that, because we cannot provide everything we need with our own hands, we should be grateful to our fellow human beings, who provide us with such necessities as food, clothing, housing, education, and entertainment. Finally, we should acknowledge that we owe a debt of gratitude to the laws that protect our lives and possessions.

Once we have recognized that we owe that fourfold debt of gratitude, Won Buddhism teaches that we should then act so as to repay that debt. We can do this by loving and honoring our parents; imitating the selfless manner in which nature provides us with the necessities of existence; treating other human beings as we would like them to treat us, and giving them what they can't provide for themselves (just as they give us things we cannot obtain for ourselves); and, finally, by obeying all just laws.

Other New Religions

Ch'ŏndogyo, Jeung San Do, Daesun Jinri-hoe, and Won Buddhism are not the only significant new indigenous religions in Korea today. Taejonggyo (the Religion of the Great Progenitor) also deserves mention, not for the size of its membership (fewer than four thousand people, according to the 2005 census), but because of the impact it has had on Korean spirituality and the Korean national holiday calendar.

Koreans celebrate National Foundation Day every year on October 3. That is the date originally established by Taejonggyo to celebrate the establishment of the legendary first Korean kingdom by Tan'gun, whom they worship as God. According to the Tan'gun myth that is the core of Taejonggyo doctrine, Tan'gun ruled so as to "broadly benefit mankind." Ever since the establishment of the Republic of Korea in 1948, "broadly benefiting mankind" has been promoted as the traditional Korean principle guiding both education and politics in the Republic of Korea.

The vast majority of Koreans today don't know just how much of what they view as Korean tradition is actually a creation of Taejonggyo, a religion that didn't emerge until the first decade of the twentieth century. In fact, few are even aware that Taejonggyo still exists and continues to promote the belief that Tan'gun, the legendary first ancestor and first ruler of the Korean people, is God. Although Taejonggyo does not have many followers, the religion continues to urge Koreans to reject foreign gods such as Jesus or Buddha in favor of their mythical ancestor.

Better known in contemporary Korea and North America is Dahn World, an offshoot of Taejonggyo. Dahn World (sometimes called Dahn Yogo) is the best known and largest of many modern internal alchemy organizations in Korea. Dahn World says it is not a religion, though it reveres the same supposedly ancient texts that Taejonggyo has enshrined in its scriptures, and it has donated statues of Tan'gun to elementary schools across Korea. Moreover, it claims that its founder, Lee Seungheun (also known as Ilchi Lee), is one of the world's foremost spiritual leaders.

Dahn World claims that while Ilchi Lee was meditating on a mountain in southern Korea in 1980, he recovered the ancient techniques of physical exercises and breathing practices that Tan'gun had created in order to broadly benefit mankind. After he began to attract many North America followers in the 1990s and moved his headquarters to Sedona, Arizona, Lee muted some of the Taejonggyo elements so visible in his early publications in Korea. Nevertheless, he still talks in the language of spirituality. In his books and speeches, he claims that the long-term goal of Dahn World is "human enlightenment and perfection." He also promotes what he calls "brain respiration" as an effective spiritual tool for individuals to become enlightened. Though Dahn World does not meet the formal definition of a religion (it has no worship services), it nevertheless should be seen as an organized manifestation of contemporary Korean spirituality.

Another Korean new religion that merits discussion, if only because it is so well-known outside of Korea, is the Unification Church of Sun Myung Moon. The Unification Church has its roots in Christianity. In fact, its original name was "the Holy Spirit Association for the Unification of World Christianity." However, it has added its own sacred writings, called *Exposition of the Divine Principle,* to the traditional Christian scriptures and has modified many traditional Christian doctrines. For example, the Unification Church teaches that Jesus was a chosen one of God but was not God himself. He was merely a messiah, sent by God to save humanity. To offer humanity complete salvation, Jesus was supposed to be married and father sinless children, ending the stain of original sin caused by the sin of Adam and Eve, the first human beings. However, Jesus was crucified before he could complete his mission. That is why God has sent a second messiah, Sun Myung Moon, to complete the mission Jesus began.

The Unification Church is no longer primarily a Korean religion; it now has a stronger presence outside of Korea than it does on the peninsula. In addition, Rev. Moon himself moved to the United States in the mid-1970s. His organization has also expanded beyond its original Christian focus. The Unification Church still exists, but it is increasingly overshadowed by Moon's larger Family Federation for World Peace and Unification.

The new religions of Korea do not claim a large share of Korea's religious population. According to the 2005 census, less than 1 percent of Koreans have a religious orientation that is not Catholic, Protestant, or mainstream Buddhist. Nevertheless, these new religions cannot be ignored if we want to paint a comprehensive picture of contemporary Korean spirituality. These new religions represent a reassertion of the validity of traditional Korean beliefs and values, even though their focus on sacred writings links them to the faith-based organized spirituality of the sort introduced to Korea by Christianity, and even though their traditional beliefs and values are supported by novel theologies. Because these new religions often claim a special spiritual role for Korea in the modern world, they reveal the close connection between Korean spirituality and Korean ethnic pride. Examining the new religions of Korea will give us insight into the state of Korean spirituality today and where it may be headed.

Nor can we ignore the multitude of other religions that were imported into Korea in the second half of the twentieth century. South Korea today is a religious supermarket in which spiritual shoppers can find almost anything they want. In addition to Catholics and Protestants, there are also Koreans who are members of the Greek Orthodox Church. There are mosques for Korea's Muslims and Baha'i meeting halls. The Chinese religion of Yigwan Dao is represented by the International Ethical Society of Korea. Japan's Tenri-kyo claims hundreds of thousands of followers, as does the Japanese lay Buddhist organization Soka Gakkai. All of these new religious organizations are evidence of how much Korea has changed over the last century. Where once diffuse spirituality dominated, now there are more Koreans who identify with a specific religious affiliation than who don't. No longer content to pursue victory over the limitations of existence as an individual without the clear and consistent guidance organized spirituality can provide, more and more Koreans have been committing themselves to the tenets and practices of specific religious organizations.

CHAPTER 6

The Spiritual Gaze in Korea

Despite the wide range of approaches to spirituality contemporary Koreans can choose from, there are some common elements that allow us to place all of them under the big tent labeled "Korean spirituality." For example, Koreans continue to pursue ways to overcome the limitations of existence as an individual, despite their theological differences. Also, Koreans generally continue to see the ethics of interpersonal interaction, especially interactions among family members, as particularly important. These legacies of the past persist today.

Traditional Korean spirituality was primarily concerned with ethics. What people did was more important than what they believed. Of special concern was how people acted toward parents, other older relatives, teachers, and leaders of their community. Koreans tended to agree on what was and what was not appropriate interpersonal behavior. Whether a person was primarily Buddhist, Confucian, or a practitioner of folk religion, the vast majority of Koreans accepted the ethical values identified with Confucianism. They believed that children should be filial, that subjects should be loyal, and that everyone should be reverent and sincere.

Different religious traditions might add additional ethical obligations to the Confucian base. Buddhism, for example, advocated respect for all forms of sentient life. The folk religion encouraged efforts to maintain proper relationships with local gods and spirits. Confucianism mandated ritual displays of respect for ancestors. Yet Koreans agreed more than they disagreed on the basic moral principles governing human behavior. Even though Christianity and some of Korea's new religions have introduced some new moral principles and ethical obligations over the last couple of centuries, even those new religious communities tend to promote the same basic traditional values. Ethical perspectives, therefore, do not provide a strong basis for differentiating the various varieties of Korean spirituality.

That is not the case with the objects of what I call the "spiritual gaze" in Korea, because Koreans traditionally tended to separate morality from theology. In the folk religion, for example, there is only a slight connection between ethics and the gods. Korea's folk gods never hand down commandments of the sort seen in the Hebrew Scriptures or the *Quran*. In mainstream Buddhism, the moral advice offered by buddhas and bodhisattvas is based on their insights into the nature of reality. Buddhist precepts are discovered rather than generated by supernatural beings. Confucianism adopts a similar attitude toward fundamental moral principles. Confucius never claimed the right to decree how human beings should behave. Instead, he said he was only teaching what sages in the past had discovered about the optimal patterns of human behavior. When Confucianism later evolved into a more philosophical Neo-Confucianism and began to focus on *li* as the ultimate normative force in the cosmos, it did not portray *li* as a lawgiver. Instead, *li* was defined as morality itself, an impersonal force that was a manifestation of the innate tendency of all phenomena in the universe to work together harmoniously.

Christianity is the only major religious tradition in Korea that grounds moral principles in the will of a supreme lawgiver. Even the new religions, though many of them have been influenced by Christianity in the ways they worship and organize themselves, do not usually present their ethical guidelines as commandments. Instead, despite their recent origins, they tend to be faithful to the traditional view that ethical principles can stand alone and that the primary role of supernatural beings is to enforce an existing moral code rather than create a new one.

Because morality and theology were not as closely intertwined in traditional Korean spirituality as they are in religious traditions that view moral codes as the manifestation of the will of a supreme being, shared ethical assumptions did not necessarily lead to shared beliefs about the grounds of those assumptions. A common moral code did not necessitate a common theology. As a result, Koreans have been free to envision an ultimate presence in the universe in a wide variety

of ways. Many Koreans, both in the past and today, have been polytheists, refusing to focus on one deity to the exclusion of others or to
limit godlike powers to one supernatural being alone. This is true not
only in the folk religion but also in popular Buddhism.

Over the last couple of centuries, polytheism has been challenged
by monotheism's insistence that there is only one God and that all
other apparent supernatural forces are either illusions or lesser spirits under the ultimate authority of the supreme ruler. Both polytheism and monotheism are anthropomorphic in that they treat their
gods as supernatural personalities with the same sort of consciousness and will that human beings enjoy. However, for well over a thousand years, ever since philosophical Buddhism gained adherents in
Korea, the anthropomorphic spiritual gaze has been challenged by a
nontheistic vision of ultimate reality. Philosophical Buddhists, Neo-
Confucians, and followers of Ch'ŏndogyo deny a human-like personality to the spiritual forces they believe are the ultimate grounds
of existence and value. Rather than an anthropomorphic spirituality, they have preferred an anthropocentric approach in which the
spiritual gaze is directed inward, toward human nature within rather
than toward a God or gods without. When they do direct their gaze
outward, they look behind the human or anthropomorphic realm to
focus on an invisible impersonal force or presence that is immanent
rather than transcendent and that is essentially the same as what they
believe is the true inner core of every human being.

Anthropomorphism and Anthropocentrism

"Anthropomorphic" and "anthropocentric" are not words that occur frequently in everyday conversation, so I should explain what I
mean when I use those terms. If you pray to a god and expect a response, then you have an anthropomorphic concept of that god, because only a conscious being can listen and respond to entreaties.
Anthropomorphic spirituality assumes the existence of supernatural
personalities with consciousness and intelligence who interact with
human beings. In anthropocentric spirituality, as I use that term,
prayers would be a waste of time, because there is no supernatural
personality to listen to those prayers. Anthropocentric spirituality is
human-centered rather than god-centered. The focus of anthropo-

centric spirituality is on self-cultivation, which means either finding the real self within (such as the buddhahood meditating monks seek to activate) or linking with impersonal forces in the cosmos (as seen in the drive by some Neo-Confucians to align their minds with the *li* of the universe).

In determining whether a belief or practice is spiritual or secular, it is irrelevant to ask whether that belief or practice is anthropomorphic or anthropocentric. An identifying feature of religion and spirituality, distinguishing them from other forms of human activity, is that they encourage practitioners to focus their gaze on some powerful being, force, or presence they need to align with in order to overcome the limitations of existence as an individual. The object of that gaze can be a supernatural personality, or it can be an impersonal force governing or sustaining the universe. It can even be an ethereal presence we locate within ourselves. For that gaze to be a spiritual gaze, the important thing is for the object of the gaze to be a source of power that can help men and women solve problems human beings cannot normally solve on their own. Usually, the object of the spiritual gaze should be invisible, immaterial, and not subject to scientific examination or technological manipulation. In other words, it must be a spiritual rather than a material object, force, or presence. An object of a spiritual gaze may have a material manifestation, but behind that manifestation there should be an invisible power or force that we can somehow come into contact with and draw strength from so that we can transcend the limitations of normal human existence. It is not necessary that this invisible power or force be endowed with a personality.

In many instances, the object of a spiritual gaze has normative or ontological force. As a normative force, it may provide a model for appropriate behavior, helping us move beyond mere personal preference in deciding what to do and how to behave. As an ontological force, it may tell us the meaning of life or what happens to us after we die, or it may be conceived as the ultimate reality that provides the foundation for the world of ordinary experience or imparts meaning to that world. Either way, the object of the spiritual gaze often provides answers for otherwise unanswerable questions.

However, the object of a spiritual gaze does not always have to have such cosmic import. Even if the object of that gaze doesn't tell us how to become a better person or provide insight into the meaning of existence or the nature of ultimate reality, it still can play a spiritual role. In popular spirituality in Korea, for example, the spiritual gaze is directed at supernatural personalities who are expected to respond to more limited requests. In the folk religion, as well as in popular Buddhism and popular Christianity, the spiritual gaze often involves requests for health, wealth, or progeny.

The Gods and Spirits of Popular Religion

The polytheism we see in both the folk tradition and popular Buddhism is a product of such specific goal-oriented spirituality. Human beings encounter many situations that cause them to feel they are not in total control of their lives; when this happens, they typically become concerned that they may suffer an unfavorable outcome. They or a family member may fall ill; they may discover that their business is failing and they are going deeply into debt; or they may be worried that their marriage is failing or that their children are not going to be able to attend the best schools or find the best possible spouse. Even in the absence of such troubling situations, there is still a lot of uncertainty in life. When we start a new job, open a new business, or enroll at a new university, we aren't sure whether we have made the right choice. Unable to see into the future, we worry about what will happen in the days, months, and years ahead.

It is at such times that many people turn to gods and spirits whom they believe possess the power to influence future events. (Spirits are slightly different from gods in that they are invisible supernatural personalities who do not wield enough power to merit the title of a god but nonetheless can do things mere human beings cannot do.) When people believe that a particular god or spirit is responsible for the problems they are experiencing, they ask that supernatural being to leave them alone. If that fails, they may ask a friendlier or more benevolent god or spirit to chase that troublesome spirit away. Even when they aren't running into any problems, people may ask a god or spirit they trust to protect them and make sure that things continue to go well for them.

In a polytheistic world, no single god or spirit addresses every is-

sue. There is a spiritual division of labor such that the proper supernatural personality to ask for help is determined by the sort of help
needed. Because polytheism denies any single god or spirit almighty
power, polytheists often ask a number of gods and spirits for help
with the same problem.

One well-known Korean scholar of folk religion has counted 273
different names for gods and spirits in Korea's traditional folk pantheon, and that doesn't include ancestors who appear in shamanic
rituals. Some of those gods and spirits have clearly defined duties. For
example, there is a group of gods that have traditionally served as village guardian deities. Their job is to keep disease-bearing spirits away
from the village while doing their best to make sure the villagers have
enough rain for their fields if it is an agricultural village, or enough
fish in their nets if fishing is the economic mainstay. The gods simply called "village gods," often enshrined in a small shrine at the entrance to a village or represented by stones stacked up alongside the
path to a village or next to a sacred tree, are never given responsibilities beyond their tutelary duties. The same limitations apply to
the two guardian generals, represented by two wooden posts called
"changsŭng," that are erected near a village entrance and carved at
the top into the shape of human heads with humorously exaggerated
features. However, those gods are not left to guard their village alone.
Many farming villages back up against a hill or mountain and therefore may also have a shrine to a protective mountain god at the rear.
A fishing village might turn to a dragon king, believed to rule over
oceans and waterways, for help and protection.

In traditional Korea, villagers would join together once a year or
so for a community ritual thanking their village gods for the help
they provided over the previous year and asking them to continue
to provide protection and assistance in the year ahead. During the
year, individual villagers would occasionally approach a tutelary deity's shrine to ask for a personal favor. Such traditional rural religious
practices have largely disappeared in recent decades (except as cultural performances to attract tourists), as Korea has gone from being
a predominantly rural society to one that is overwhelmingly urban.

Similarly, the gods and spirits who dwelled in various parts of a
traditional home have also largely disappeared. In the high-rise con-

dominiums where many Koreans now make their homes, the kitchen no longer has a dirt floor that separates it from other rooms in the house. Nor do inhabitants have to go across an open courtyard to reach the toilet, as they had to do in traditional village houses. When all the rooms have the same type of floor and are right next to each other, there is no need for the eight or nine different gods who populated a traditional house. With no hearths, gates, or outhouses to guard, traditional guardian spirits such as the outhouse god or the god of the hearth have no employment opportunities in modern urban dwellings. Even the traditional grandmother goddess of fertility and childbirth, *samsin,* is not needed as much as she used to be, now that women can turn to a physician for help in giving birth and raising their children.

Gods that have homes of their own outside of rural houses and villages have fared better. Most Buddhist temple complexes, in addition to their large worship halls with statues and paintings of Buddhist deities and spirits, have a small shrine up the hill behind the main buildings. That shrine houses either a sole mountain god or the "three sages" (described below). Visitors to a large Buddhist temple complex will often stop by this shrine to ask that he (or she; many mountain gods are female) protect them while they are on that god's mountain. Married women may also visit the shrine of a mountain god to ask for help in bearing a son. Particularly impressive mountains will have an especially powerful mountain god who was sometimes approached by government officials in traditional Korea for help in dealing with national crises. In recent decades, I haven't seen any government officials approach a mountain god shrine as a true supplicant rather than as part of a reenactment of a traditional ritual. However, I have witnessed many ordinary Koreans walk up to a shrine, stop, face the shrine's front doors, and bow in a brief prayer.

The presence of a mountain god inside a shrine is usually indicated by a brightly colored painting of an old man with a long white beard, or, in some cases, a middle-aged woman. Whether male or female, a mountain god is always accompanied by a tiger. That distinguishes the mountain god from two other figures that may appear in paintings hung alongside the mountain god painting in a Three Sages shrine. One figure, the Big Dipper god, is actually depicted as seven identical gods, usually male, sometimes female, but always shown wearing Buddhist clothing. The seven figures in the Big Dipper god painting represent the seven stars in the Big Dipper constellation. There is a popular misconception in Korea that the Big Dipper god, like the mountain god, is an intrusion of Korean folk religion into Buddhist sacred space, but that is incorrect. There were shrines to the Big Dipper god in both Buddhist temples and Daoist shrines in China before they appeared in Korea. Koreans may have also learned from the Chinese that the Big Dipper God is an appropriate god to pray to if you want to live a long time or if you want to add a baby boy to your family. The Big Dipper God is so important that at many temples it has its own shrine instead of having to share one with the mountain god.

The third figure in a shrine to the three sages is usually the "old hermit-sage." The old hermit usually looks similar to a male mountain god, except his beard is not as long and he doesn't have a tiger by his side or at his feet. He may represent a monk who has retreated into the mountains to meditate in isolation but more likely is a depiction of a mountain-dwelling immortal of the sort that has been a part of Korean folk tradition for well over a millennium. Mountain immortals are not actually immortal; nor are they gods or spirits in the usual sense. Instead, they are human beings who have learned how to slow the normal aging process so dramatically that they are able to live for hundreds of years. According to folk tales, mountain immortals are able to ride the wind and otherwise escape the normal limitations of human material existence. Some Koreans believe that there are still such "immortals" hiding away in the mountains to this day and enjoying a trouble-free existence. Normally, such immortals are referred to as "sŏn," but a few of them rise to the level of lower-level gods and are called "sinsŏn" (divine immortals). One such divine immortal is Tan'gun, the legendary first king of the first Korean kingdom, who abdicated after more than one thousand years on the throne and withdrew to a nearby mountain to serve as the god of that mountain.

Tan'gun is also one of the many gods who may appear on the paintings a shaman hangs on the wall behind the altar in the shrine she maintains in her home. Each shaman will honor only a few gods in that way. Because each shaman has her own favorite gods, there is a great variety of gods who appear on shaman altar walls and either appear in or are appealed to in shaman rituals. The same scholar who counted 273 different gods and spirits in Korea's folk pantheon says that at least 115 of them appear either on shaman walls or on the walls of shrines. That still leaves another 158 gods and spirits who do not appear in the religious art of the folk tradition. What role is left for them to play in folk spirituality?

Most of those unrepresented deities and spirits, along with many who are depicted in paintings and statues, appear in shaman rituals, either as the object of the shaman's prayers and entreaties or as a god or spirit summoned by the shaman to interact with the shaman or her clients. The names of these gods and spirits vary from region to region in Korea, and even from shaman to shaman in the same region, as do the specific functions they serve. Nevertheless, we can classify those gods and spirits into several categories.

There are gods who dwell in the skies above. They often assume responsibility for fate, life spans, and the weather. They include the gods of the sun, the moon, and the stars (including but not limited to the Big Dipper). Among them are Tan'gun (when he is not serving as a mountain god) and the deity Indra, borrowed from Hinduism by way of Buddhism, under the name of Chesŏk. (Chesŏk is sometimes depicted as three identical figures wearing Buddhist clothing.) The Daoist Jade Emperor also makes an appearance in shaman rituals once in a while, as does a deity simply called the "celestial god" or "celestial king."

Despite the widespread belief in South Korea today that Korean folk tradition has long included worship of Hananim (the One God) or Hanŭnim (the Lord in Heaven Above), there is no evidence that such a term was used for a monotheistic God before Christianity began using it that way or that there were any monotheistic tendencies in Korea's folk tradition at all. Korea's folk tradition assumes that a number of gods dwell in heaven above. Moreover, though they may be more powerful than most terrestrial deities, none of the celestial deities are seen as a supreme being. Instead, the celestial gods are simply numbered among the supernatural personalities of varying degrees of power and responsibility that Koreans have worshipped from time immemorial.

In addition to celestial deities, there are a number of types of earthbound deities in the folk pantheon. They include gods of the soil, who share with celestial deities responsibility for success or failure in agriculture, as well as gods such as the house-site god and the village guardian god whose primary duty is to protect the areas around them. Also there are road gods who protect travelers, waterway gods who are supposed to protect those who sail upon them as well as to provide them a bountiful catch, fire gods, gods of the wind, tree gods, rock gods, door gods, and directional gods. The last are usually depicted as five fierce-looking warriors who keep harmful spirits and other dangerous influences away from us by guarding the five directions: north, south, east, west, and center.

There are also a number of divine generals a shaman can call upon to help her chase troublesome spirits away. Among the powerful spirits a shaman can summon is the "general who rides the fodder-chopper." A charismatic shaman often shows that she has been possessed by that powerful spirit by standing without shoes on the sharpened edge of a fodder-chopping knife. When possessed by such a powerful divinity, she can tell lesser spirits what to do. Among the troublesome spirits she may chase away in this manner are dangerous spirits that cause serious diseases. A shaman would probably not bother to ask the help of a divine general if she were only dealing with a minor nuisance such as a goblin-like Tokkaebi, who is more of a prankster than a threat.

Most of the gods and spirits mentioned above, with the exception of Tokkaebi and divine generals, are examples of anthropomorphic animism, which is necessary for the shaman or other supplicant to be able to negotiate with the natural forces and phenomena that affect human lives. However, not all of the spirits in the folk pantheon are examples of animism. Others are gods who were gods from the beginning (such as the divine generals) or were once animals or human beings but have now been deified. Aside from various horse gods, tiger gods, and snake gods (an indicator of household prosperity), most such folk deities and spirits didn't need to be anthropomorphized because they were either human or human-like when they first appeared in Korea. All they needed, if they were not already gods, was to be deified.

Many Korean folk gods are dead people. They include kings, queens, princesses, generals (such as Gwan Yu, the famous general from the Chinese tale "Romance of the Three Kingdoms"), and the wives of generals. However, shamans also enshrine powerful long-dead government officials and the spirit simply called "the first Korean shaman." They also import gods and other powerful spirits from Buddhism. Chesŏk is not the only Buddhist deity to appear on shaman walls. The Healing Buddha is particularly popular among shamans, as is the bodhisattva Kwanŭm. Famous monks are also sometimes raised posthumously to the level of powerful spirits. Even the historical Buddha, Sakyamuni, shows up on shaman walls or in shaman rites every once in a while.

The folk pantheon is not static. As living conditions change, so does our need for supernatural assistance in successfully navigating those changed conditions. There are now gods in charge of protecting automobiles and even gods who specialize in protecting automobile engines only. As more Koreans have left the farm, moved into towns or cities, and started small businesses, new gods have appeared to help those small businesspeople succeed and become wealthy.

Furthermore, gods and powerful spirits are not the only personalities who appear in shaman rituals. Charismatic shamans are often called upon when Koreans want to contact a recently deceased loved one. I once witnessed a ritual held on the third anniversary of the sudden death of a young man in an automobile accident. His parents and his sister hired a shaman to arrange for them to say their goodbyes to him, something they had not been able to do at the time of his death due to the sudden, unexpected nature of his passing. As I watched, the shaman (a woman at least fifty years old) was possessed by the spirit of that young man and talked to them. They responded as though they were actually conversing with that dead family member. His sister even apologized for teasing him when he was young. When the possession was drawing to a close and his spirit announced he had to return to the realm of the dead, his parents and his sister said tearful good-byes.

Sudden death, especially in the case of someone too young to leave any descendants behind to care for his spirit after his death, creates unhappy wandering spirits sometimes called "hungry ghosts" because there is no one to offer them ritual food through ancestor memorial services. Those spirits often wander around near where they once lived, trying to gain the attention of family, friends, and neighbors. Unfortunately, the touch of the dead, even if it is well intentioned, causes problems for the living, including financial and health problems. One of the many roles shamans played in traditional Korea was to contact those spirits, convince them that they had not been forgotten, tell them that ritual food would be left out for them on a regular basis, and ask them to please leave the living alone. Shamans continue to play that role today, though less frequently than they did in the past.

Buddhist Polytheism

Even the most powerful gods in the folk pantheon are not usually as powerful as the gods available in Korea's popular Buddhist tradition. One indication of that greater potency is the fact that gods in the folk tradition are not often represented by statues. Instead, they are usually depicted in two-dimensional paintings, if at all. However, powerful buddhas and bodhisattvas appear not only in paintings but also in large, awe-inspiring statues housed in temple buildings that are much more impressive than the small rooms in which gods of the folk tradition usually are found. Also, there are a lot fewer buddhas and bodhisattvas than there are folk gods and spirits, so their power is not spread as thinly.

Nevertheless, there is still enough variety in the halls of Buddhist temples for us to say that Buddhism as practiced by the average lay practitioner is essentially polytheistic, in that visitors to a temple will acknowledge the presence of many deities and usually will pray to several of them. Visitors to a large temple complex will notice some of those gods as they pass through the gates that separate the sacred space of the temple from the secular world. Standing guard at the second of what are usually three gates into a temple complex are four gods imported from Hinduism, two on the left and two on the right. Those gods are often represented by large statues of fierce-looking warriors crushing with their legs some almost-as-powerful opponents of Buddhism.

Once a visitor enters into the temple proper, she will find even more powerful deities awaiting her prayers, bows, and prostrations. Different temples honor different buddhas in the main halls, but they normally draw from a limited range. The main hall usually has three large statues, with the center statue being either the Cosmic Buddha, Amitabha, the Healing Buddha, or Sakyamuni, the title of the man from South Asia who became the Buddha, "the enlightened one." Depending on who the central figure is, the other two major statues in the main hall may be other buddhas or bodhisattvas. In addition, there may also be smaller statues of bodhisattvas.

Bodhisattvas, as we saw in chapter 3, are those who are so spiritually advanced that they are ready to escape entirely from this world

The main hall at Yakch'ŏn-sa temple on Cheju Island. The Cosmic Buddha, in the center, is flanked by Amitabha and the Healing Buddha. The two smaller statues off to the side are the bodhisattvas of wisdom and compassion. Author photo.

of transitory and therefore frustrating phenomena; but they have decided to postpone their own release in order to help other sentient beings follow the same path they have followed. They are often depicted as assistants to more powerful buddhas. However, in the minds of many lay Buddhists, a bodhisattva has as much power to help them as a full buddha does. A particularly popular bodhisattva, not only in Korea but in the rest of East Asia as well, is the bodhisattva of compassion (Kwanŭm or Kwanseŭm in Korean). This bodhisattva is sometimes seated next to Amitabha but is also sometimes given a hall or freestanding statue of her own. (Considered a male bodhisattva in India and Tibet, she is usually thought of as female in China and Korea.) To make matters more confusing, a couple of full buddhas also appear in temples as bodhisattvas. The Healing Buddha is often the bodhisattva of healing instead, though he only gets his own hall when he is depicted as a full buddha. Another bodhisattva who is also sometimes portrayed as a full buddha is the Buddha of the Future.

With this many different Buddhist deities to choose from, how do practitioners decide whom to pray to? Visitors to a temple complex do not usually pray before only one buddha or bodhisattva. Instead, they will visit several halls and pray before the buddha or bodhisattva that is the main figure in each hall, or even before all the buddhas and bodhisattvas in that hall. However, they may give more attention to one buddha or bodhisattva than another. Amitabha will garner most of their attention if they want to take advantage of Amitabha's promise to help those with sufficient faith but insufficient merit gain rebirth into his paradise. If they have a medical problem that they feel needs a buddha's attention, they will focus their prayers and attention on the Healing Buddha. Sakyamuni is for those who want to imitate his example of achieving enlightenment on this earth. And the Cosmic Buddha is for those who feel the need for the buddha who represents cosmic power.

In most temples, Sakyamuni will have the place of honor in the main hall, but Amitabha will either be at his side or in another hall off to the side, the "hall of perfect bliss," an allusion to the paradise Amitabha promises to those who sincerely trust in him. Temple complexes also will have a separate hall for the bodhisattva who has

pledged to help the newly dead achieve the best possible rebirth. His
hall is called the Judgment Hall, because he shares that hall with the
Ten Judges who determine where a person will spend his or her next
life based on that person's behavior in the life just ended. Those who
have recently lost a loved one will visit that hall to pray for the Ten
Judges to be merciful.

With so many buddhas and bodhisattvas in one temple complex,
it is not surprising that sometimes lay believers are not sure which
particular Buddhist deity they are praying to. Once I hiked eight
hundred meters up a mountain outside of the city of Taegu to see a
huge statue carved into the face of the mountain near its summit. A
large concrete platform had been placed in front of the statue to allow
worshippers to perform the multiple prostrations that are a common
way for Buddhists to pray. Worshippers are supposed to chant the
name of the buddha or bodhisattva they are praying to as they make
their prostrations. I had been told before I started my hike that this
particular statue was a representation of the Healing Buddha. Several
of the people on the platform with me confirmed that I had climbed
the right path by chanting "hail the Healing Buddha" as they bowed.
However, others chanted "hail the Buddha of the Future," and still
others chanted "hail the bodhisattva of compassion." No one seemed
to be bothered by this apparent confusion over which buddha or bodhisattva that statue was supposed to represent. I was also told that
this particular buddha or bodhisattva, no matter who he or she is,
will not only respond to requests for help with medical problems but
is also very good at helping the children of supplicants enter a good
university and will often respond affirmatively to requests for help
dealing with financial or family problems.

Philosophical Buddhism and Monodevotionalism

Monks who represent the more philosophical strain of Korean Buddhism offer several explanations for this apparent inconsistency and
confusion in Korean Buddhist practice. According to one explanation, the Buddha is the only lord, creator, and savior of the universe.
However, he has manifested himself to humanity in a number of different ways. Sakyamuni is one manifestation of this cosmic buddha,

but so are Amitabha and the Healing Buddha. This monotheistic explication says that no matter which buddha or bodhisattva someone prays to and bows before, they are worshipping the one Buddha. Whether a Buddhist concentrates on one statue in a temple complex or bows in worship before all them is not important. What is important is that they worship at least one buddha, demonstrating that they know there is a supernatural presence with power much greater than their own.

Another explanation, one popular with Buddhist philosophers, does away with theism entirely. A core principle of Buddhist philosophy, as we saw in chapter 3, is that the world of experience — because it is transitory, and everything in it is brought into existence by something else — is ultimately unreal. However, underlying this unreal world of dependent transitory phenomena is Buddha nature, undifferentiated all-encompassing thusness. There is nothing truly real outside of Buddha nature, nor is there anything in Buddha nature that can be distinguished from something else in Buddha nature. If this denial of all differentiation as essentially unreal is applied to buddhas and bodhisattvas, then the worship of one buddha or of many buddhas and bodhisattvas is worship of an illusion, because a buddha is ultimately no different from anything else in the universe.

What, then, is a sincere Buddhist philosopher to do? The answer is to study, meditate, chant, discipline your body, do whatever you have to do to see through the illusory veil that is the world of everyday experience and awaken (become enlightened) to the undifferentiated thusness underlying phenomenal experience. However, Buddhist philosophers also recognize that not everyone, not even every Buddhist monk or nun, is capable of escaping from the normal way of looking at the world as divided into separate and distinct entities. Therefore, they encourage those who are less advanced spiritually to focus their attention on buddhas and bodhisattvas as a way to develop attitudes of compassion and of trust in something greater than themselves. Such spiritual attitudes, philosophers believe, will help them overcome the excessive focus on the self that is the root of all evil. Once they have transcended the narrow perspective that makes them think and act as though the universe revolves around them, they have taken the first steps toward developing—if not in this life, then perhaps in the next—an ability to also transcend any false hopes of gaining permanent satisfaction in this world. Once they have achieved that attitude of nonattachment, they will have earned release from the suffering that is caused by the search for permanence in an impermanent world, and they will no longer need the crutch of theism that helped them navigate the lower reaches of the path to salvation.

To readers raised in religious traditions that emphasize doctrinal conformity, this willingness to tolerate different attitudes toward the Buddha, buddhas, and bodhisattvas may seem strange. However, most Buddhist leaders do not feel compelled to impose theological uniformity on the Buddhist community, because they believe that what Buddhists believe is less important than what they do. As long as their spiritual gaze—whether it is polytheistic, monotheistic, or nontheistic—helps them rise above egocentrism, it is leading them in the right direction. Even though prayers to a particular buddha for a specific benefit, such as healing or success on university exams, may seem to be a contradiction of the ultimate Buddhist goal of outgrowing the illusion that the individual self is real, such prayers are permitted because they are seen as early steps toward ultimate enlightenment.

The first step is the recognition that there are powers greater than our own and that if we want to overcome the limits of our existence as an individual, we have to trust in and align ourselves with a greater power. Furthermore, Buddhism encourages practitioners to cultivate a sense of compassion, which can be expressed in the earliest stages merely by praying for others rather than for our personal self-interest. Compassion can be manifested as prayers for the health of a family member or for the academic success of a son or daughter. Even if we pray to a buddha or a bodhisattva to help someone close to us, such as a relative, we have made the first step toward universal compassion and selflessness by asking for something that doesn't benefit us exclusively. In doing so, we have moved away from the exclusive focus on ourselves that is the ultimate cause of suffering in this world. Therefore, filling the halls of Buddhist temples with statues is not only acceptable, it is actually advisable, because the vast majority of human beings alive at any one time are still at the lower levels of spiritual advancement and need all the help they can get to begin their upward climb.

There is one Buddhist order, however, that is consistently faithful to the philosophy that reality is undifferentiated. Won Buddhism is a new Buddhist religion and consequently is not bound to the traditional acceptance of statues and anthropomorphic deities within temple walls. Instead, Won Buddhism carries Buddhist nontheism to its logical conclusion. As was noted in the preceding chapter, there are no statues or even paintings of buddhas or bodhisattvas in Won Buddhist temples. Instead, on the front walls of the rooms in which Won Buddhists gather every Sunday for religious services, there is only a large circle. Won Buddhists focus their spiritual gaze on that circle, which they call "Ilwonsang."

Ilwonsang could be literally translated as "the symbol *(sang)* of a perfect circle *(ilwon),*" but it means much more than that to Won Buddhists. It is a depiction in graphic form of impersonal, undiffer-

Sunday service in a Won Buddhist temple. Photo courtesy of the World Headquarters of Won Buddhism.

entiated thusness. According to the scriptures of Won Buddhism, the perfect circle "is the original source of all things in the universe, the mind-seal of all the buddhas and sages, and the original nature of all sentient beings; the realm where there is no discrimination regarding great and small, being and nonbeing; the realm where there is no change amid arising and ceasing, coming and going; the realm where wholesome and unwholesome karmic retribution has ceased; the realm where language, names, and characteristics are utterly void." Won Buddhists also say that Ilwonsang is a depiction of the buddha-body that constitutes the universe. However, they refuse to depict that buddha-body anthropomorphically, for, they argue, that would add form to what is formless.

Won Buddhists focus their spiritual gaze on Ilwonsang with an intensity that can be called religious devotion. However, just like some of the more philosophical Buddhists, they are not monotheists. A more appropriate way to describe their spiritual gaze would be to call it "monodevotion." And even when they focus on Ilwonsang, they also look within. Won Buddhist scriptures tell us to learn to recognize and activate our true inner nature, which is as perfect and complete, as fully impartial and selfless, as *ilwon*. The core of spiritual practice for Won Buddhists is to nurture that inner nature so that it becomes the mind and heart that generates their thoughts and directs their actions as they go about their daily lives. Won Buddhism can therefore be characterized as anthropocentric monodevotion, and in that respect it resembles mainstream meditative Buddhism, which also focuses on the Buddha nature within rather than an anthropomorphic deity without.

Neo-Confucian Anthropocentrism and the Challenge of Christianity

Neo-Confucianism falls under the same category as Won Buddhism and meditative Buddhism. Like them, it does not have a supernatural personality as the focus of its spiritual gaze, and it focuses on the activation and cultivation of true human nature rather than on worship of some external deity. However, Neo-Confucians didn't talk about Buddha nature. Instead, they focused their spiritual attention on *li,* the cosmic network of appropriate relationships, and on *ki,* the matter and energy that provide substance and motion to the cosmos. Though the original Confucian Classics from more than two thousand years ago spoke at times of heaven and a Lord on High as though they were endowed with consciousness and will, Neo-Confucianism demoted such anthropomorphic discourse to the level of metaphor. Morality as the organizing principle of the universe (for that is what Neo-Confucian *li* amounted to) did not need a personality.

In the Neo-Confucian worldview, *li* was more than just the impartial cosmic network of appropriate relationships that directed everything in the universe into patterns of selfless harmonious interaction (when it was allowed to operate unhindered). *Li* was also the heart-and-mind within every human being that told us how to think and behave appropriately, that is to say, impartially, sincerely, reverently, and without regard for personal self-interest. Neo-Confucian spiritual practice focused on clearing away impediments, such as the selfish thoughts *ki* generated, so that our true human nature, our virtuous heart-and-mind of *li,* could assume its rightful commanding role. Meditation to calm our emotions, ritual to calm the mind and body, and the study of Confucian writings were practices Neo-Confucians used to direct their spiritual gaze toward the impersonal unifying network that governed the universe and should also govern our thoughts and actions.

Though Neo-Confucians would sometimes "pray" to heaven above, they normally did so with the full understanding that heaven could not hear their pleas. Instead, they expected their display of devotion to the ideal of selfless cooperation that was *li*—and that sometimes was referred to metaphorically as "heaven"—to resonate with the cosmic network of appropriate interaction and rectify whatever imbalance, such as a drought or an epidemic, had stimulated that prayer. Neo-Confucians did not worship heaven or *li* in the same way that theists and polytheists worshipped their gods. Neo-Confucian spirituality was anthropocentric rather than anthropomorphic, focused on activating true human nature within and aligning with impersonal normative principles without, rather than glorifying or beseeching some supernatural personality.

Christianity and Anthropomorphic Monotheism

When Neo-Confucians encountered Christianity in the eighteenth century, most of them were appalled. At that point in their history, Koreans were familiar with both anthropomorphic polytheism and anthropocentric monodevotionalism. The Neo-Confucian ruling elite associated polytheism with the uneducated masses that frequented shamans and temples. Educated men were supposed to be above such anthropomorphism and focus their spiritual gaze on impersonal *li* instead. Nevertheless, they could tell that the books introducing Catholicism to Korea were written by educated men. They also noticed that the first converts to Catholicism came mostly from the educated class. This surprised them, because those Catholic books clearly taught anthropomorphic monotheism, a combination that Neo-Confucians were not well acquainted with but which did not seem suitable for the well educated.

To an orthodox Neo-Confucian, the notion of a divine personality reigning in heaven above was completely irrational. How could Catholics, who appeared to be intelligent and well educated, believe in a God they couldn't see or hear? Even worse, Catholic theology appeared to have immoral implications. To Neo-Confucians, the focus of a spiritual gaze should be a model for moral thought and behavior, impartial and unselfish, like *li*. Mainstream Neo-Confucians insisted that it was morally unacceptable to worship a God who rewarded those who worshipped and obeyed him and punished those who didn't, because such a divine personality displayed a favoritism that was the very opposite of the impartiality and concern for the common good that Neo-Confucians enshrined as the highest moral good.

One eighteenth-century Korean Neo-Confucian was particularly mystified by the Catholic insistence that God, a supernatural personality, was also the supreme good. He countered that it was an insult to the supreme good to say that it would select one people out of the many different peoples on earth to be his chosen people and then favor them by sending his son to dwell among them, and only them. Such a display of favoritism contradicts the Christian claim that their God is the very model and even the source of morality.

Another scholar reacted to what he read in Catholic books by insisting that a truly moral God would not get so angry with those who disobeyed his instructions that he would condemn them to eternal damnation. Instead, a just God would take the time to teach those who misbehaved to behave better in the future.

Such sharp criticisms of the anthropomorphic monotheism of Christianity persuaded most of the Koreans who read Catholic books in the eighteenth and nineteenth centuries that Christianity was not for them. However, starting at the end of the eighteenth century, a few become convinced that the morality of interpersonal interaction that was at the heart of Confucianism was better supported by a God with an anthropomorphic personality than by an impersonal philosophical abstraction such as *li*. These first Korean Christians appear to have been particularly sensitive to human moral frailty, humanity's inability to consistently adhere to the demands of its own moral codes. They were drawn to Christianity by more than the usual religious motives of seeking access to supernatural assistance in order to overcome health, financial, or family problems. They became convinced that God would reward their belief in him with a divine grace that would enable them to overcome innate human moral weakness and become better human beings.

Those few who were attracted to Catholic monotheism managed to establish a small Catholic community that remained intact over the course of the nineteenth century despite repeated persecution. When the social system that had supported Neo-Confucianism began to erode under the impact of modern civilization at the end of the nineteenth century, space opened up for the Protestant version of Christianity to enter Korea as well. In the twentieth century, though the hold of Confucian values on the Korean heart remained firm, the Neo-Confucian philosophical underpinning of those values faded into irrelevance. In its place, Christianity became the dominant spiritual force on the peninsula, changing not only the way Koreans viewed Christianity but also the way they viewed monotheism (including anthropomorphic monotheism) in general.

The Christian concept of God is radically different from the way Koreans had viewed gods before they encountered Christianity. Although the Christian God is the supreme being, his Christian followers believe they can talk to him, and he responds. In other words, it was possible for Korean Christians to have a personal relationship with God. That was a novel idea for Koreans. Before Christianity was introduced to Korea, the only gods Koreans normally encountered were the gods of the folk tradition, who might have been gods but who were definitely not supreme beings. Korea's indigenous gods were only a little more powerful than humans and did not even come close to the dignity and majesty of the Christian God.

This idea of a personal relationship with God has proven very attractive to Koreans, so much so that today, three out of every ten South Koreans is a Christian. Even some of the non-Christian religions of Korea have been influenced by Christian monotheism and by Christian notions of the importance of personal encounters with God.

Ch'ŏndogyo and Anthropocentric Monotheism

Ch'ŏndogyo, as mentioned in chapter 5, is the oldest of Korea's new religions. It appeared eighty years after the first Catholic community was formed in Korea and almost twenty-five years before the first Protestant missionary began preaching on the Korean peninsula. To the extent that Ch'ŏndogyo is monotheistic, it represents a break with Korean tradition and shows the influence of Christianity. However, the way it conceives of that one god shows a strong influence from Neo-Confucian philosophy. Though Ch'oe may have reported that he talked with the lord of heaven, the patriarchs who systematized his teachings after his death said he was speaking metaphorically. They insisted that Hanullim was not a supernatural personality in the sky above but an impersonal presence that filled the universe, including our own hearts and minds. The monotheism of the founder shaded into monodevotionalism under his successors.

In the writings of the patriarchs who followed Ch'oe, God appears as the animating force in the universe, a force that we can experience personally when we ask ultimate energy to fill our hearts with spiritual energy. We should also recognize that this force is present not only in ourselves but also in all other human beings, as well as in all other animate objects in the universe. This stress on the impersonal and universally pervasive nature of the absolute may reflect Neo-Confucian influence, but it is not Neo-Confucianism. Neo-Confucians never had any personal encounters with *li,* their abstract absolute. However, neither is Hanullim the sort of supernatural personality seen in popular Buddhism or in Korea's folk religion. Instead, Hanullim is an impersonal force that we can experience personally, just as Christians can have a personal relationship with Jesus Christ. In Ch'ŏndogyo, instead of attending revival meetings of the sort so popular among Korean Christians, believers have their personal encounter with the divine by chanting over and over again the incantation that Hanullim revealed to Ch'oe Cheu, as discussed in chapter 5.

That incantation begins with the lines "Ultimate Energy being all around me, I pray that I feel that Energy within me here and now. Recognizing that God is within me, I will be transformed." Those two lines affirm the Ch'ŏndogyo belief that God is ultimate energy, more *ki* than *li.* However, ultimate energy in Ch'ŏndogyo has the same moral import that *li* has in Neo-Confucianism. In Ch'ŏndogyo, ultimate energy is the force that links everything in the universe and makes harmonious cooperation possible. Hanullim is not a God existing above and beyond us; Hanulllim is the power we experience within ourselves to join with the rest of the universe to continue the process of creation and build a better, more harmonious world. This belief is expressed in the Ch'ŏndogyo principle that every human being has a spark of the divine within him or her.

The anthropocentric nature of the God of Ch'ŏndogyo is made even more explicit in the writings of the third patriarch, Son Pyŏnghŭi (1861–1921). In an essay included in the scriptures of Ch'ŏndogyo, Son writes, "The Lord Above is nothing other than our own minds. Heaven and Earth are also our own minds, and so are all the phenomena in the world. When we talk about 'serving the Lord of Heaven,' what we are talking about is maintaining respectful awareness of the spark of the divine within our own bodies."

Non-Christian Trinitarian Monotheism

Ch'ŏndogyo's use of monotheistic language to describe Hanullim, a god different from any god Koreans had worshipped before the nineteenth century, shows that the Christian introduction of anthropomorphic monotheism transformed Korean spirituality. We can see further evidence of this transformation in two indigenous Korean religions that appeared fifty years after the birth of Ch'ŏndogyo. Both Taejonggyo and Daesun Jinri-hoe have their roots in the first decade of the twentieth century. Neither are Christian religions, yet both now teach a trinitarian monotheism of the sort that Koreans first encountered in Christianity.

Taejonggyo, the "Religion of the Great Progenitor," proclaims that it is the revival of the ancient religion of Korea, back when Tan'gun ruled over the Korean people. According to the Taejonggyo version of Korean history, the worship of Tan'gun was the national religion of Korea for three thousand years, from the time of Tan'gun's reign until the Mongol invasions of the thirteenth century. However, the destruction of much of Korea's traditional culture by the Mongols, combined with machinations by proponents of the imported religions of Buddhism and Neo-Confucianism, pushed worship of Tan'gun underground and out of sight, until it was revived by an anti-Japanese nationalist named Na Ch'ŏl (1863–1916) in 1909.

The defining tenet of Taejonggyo is that Koreans do not need to worship any foreign gods because they have a God of their own. That God, Tan'gun, is also known as Hanŏllim and Hanbaegŏm. All three names are pure Korean and cannot be written in Chinese, unlike the Chinese names for Confucian sages and Buddhist deities and the Sino-Korean names for many of the gods and spirits of the folk tradition. That, according to Taejonggyo, is one reason why Tan'gun is a more appropriate god for Koreans than any imported gods.

Not only does Tan'gun have three native Korean names, he is a member of a divine trinity whose names are drawn from what Koreans believe is the founding myth of their nation and people. According to that myth, a celestial deity named Hwanin dispatched a son named Hwanung to earth to "broadly benefit humanity" and provide human beings with a benevolent government. Hwanung knew that human beings needed a ruler more human than he was, so he lay with a bear who had been transformed into a human female. The union begat Tan'gun, who proceeded to rule over the first Korean kingdom for more than one thousand years. Though most Koreans do not read a trinitarian theology into that myth, Taejonggyo teaches that Hwanin, Hwanung, and Tan'gun are actually three persons in one god. (According to Taejonggyo, the trinity of Christian belief is a copy of the much older trinity of Korea's ancient religion.) Those three persons represent the different functions of the one supreme being. Hwanin is God as creator, Hwanung is God as educator, and Tan'gun is God as ruler. Despite their trinitarian beliefs, Taejonggyo churches have only one material representation of the god they worship. They say they need a statue of Tan'gun only because when they worship him they also worship his father and his grandfather. (In a sign of the continued power of patriarchy in modern Korea, Tan'gun's bear mother is never worshipped.)

The other major non-Christian trinitarian theology in Korea is found in the teachings of Daesun Jinri-hoe (the Association Promoting the Truth Promulgated during the Great Peregrinations of the Supreme Lord Above). Daesun Jinri-hoe is the largest of several Korean new religions focused on the worship of Kang Chŭngsan, whom they believe was the incarnation in the human world of the supreme lord of the highest heaven. Daesun Jinri-hoe is the only member of the Chŭngsan family of religions to develop a trinitarian theology, and it has done so fairly recently.

According to Daesun Jinri-hoe, there are many gods and spirits in heaven, including various buddhas and bodhisattvas as well as Jesus Christ and even Matteo Ricci, the famous Jesuit missionary to China. Also included among the gods and spirits in heaven are the progenitors of various ethnic groups and family lines. Because Daesun Jinri-hoe recognizes the existence of so many supernatural personalities, it would seem at first glance that the religion is polytheistic. However, Daesun Jinri-hoe insists that it emphasizes the worship of the greatest god of them all and therefore should be classified as monotheistic. According to Daesun Jinri-hoe, Kang Chŭngsan was the incarnation of the ruler of the spirit realm above, the one and only God who could tell the other gods what to do, the one and only God who was also the creator and ruler of the human realm below. He alone is worthy of being called the supreme lord of the highest heaven. The record of what he did and said when he walked on Korean soil serves as the sacred scripture of Daesun Jinri-hoe, playing the same role that the New Testament plays in Christian organizations. Because Daesun Jinri-hoe says only one god should be the ultimate focus of our spiritual gaze and has based its doctrines on the teachings of their supreme lord, monotheism does appear to be an apt label for this religion.

Nevertheless, one powerful group within Daesun Jinri-hoe also teaches that there are actually three divine persons, just as Christianity and Taejonggyo do. However, the three members of the Daesun Jinri-hoe trinity are all actual individuals who lived in Korea in the twentieth century. Kang was a real person who "returned to heaven" in 1909 after he had completed his mission on this earth. That mission was to teach humanity the "rites of cosmic renewal." When performed correctly, regularly, and sincerely, this ritual will hasten the end of the current universe of constant conflict and rampant injustice, ushering in the Great Transformation that will create a new universe of peace, justice, and universal harmonious cooperation. The supreme lord descended from heaven and became Kang Chǔngsan to teach humanity how to put an end to the many problems human beings face and replace this vale of tears with a paradise.

Kang himself did not establish a formal religious organization to ensure that his rituals were performed regularly and properly. The second member of the trinity, Cho Ch'ŏlje (1895–1958), did that by establishing the Way of the Great Ultimate a couple of decades after Kang left this earth. When Cho "returned to heaven" in 1958, his disciple Park Han'gyŏng (1918–1996) left the Way of the Great Ultimate to found Daesun Jinri-hoe. Today Kang, Cho, and Park are enshrined together in some Daesun Jinri-hoe worship halls because they are believed to have displayed supreme wisdom, infinite grace, and creative power as they went about the task of preparing humanity for the Great Transformation.

Though Daesun Jinri-hoe is theocentric in that it defines itself by its worship of the supreme lord above and its adherence to the rituals, ethics, and doctrines Kang Chǔngsan taught, it could also be called somewhat anthropocentric. Its anthropocentrism comes through in Daesun Jinri-hoe's description of the universe after the Great Transformation. According to Daesun Jinri-hoe, human beings are now living in a universe controlled by the gods. However, the gods, including God himself, plan to step out of the way after the Great Transformation. In the paradisiacal realm human beings will inhabit after the Great Transformation, there will be no poverty, no disease, no conflict, and no injustice. Because they will have a problem-free existence, men and women will not need divine assistance anymore.

The Daesun Jinri-hoe description of the paradise that awaits humanity is quite different from the release from existence as a separate and distinct individual that philosophical Buddhists see as the goal of their spiritual endeavors. However, both philosophical Buddhists and members of Daesun Jinri-hoe believe that human beings will outgrow their need for gods. Neo-Confucians would agree. Christians, participants in the folk tradition, and religious Buddhists, among others, would not agree. Their religious imagination has no room for a godless universe, even in the far distant future. Nevertheless, Koreans across the spiritual spectrum share the same basic assumption about the role of gods, benevolent spirits, or other objects of their spiritual gaze. Whether the focus of their spiritual gaze is a supernatural personality or an impersonal cosmic moral force, whether their spiritual practices are theocentric or anthropocentric, Koreans assume that they have to link up or align themselves with some power greater than their own in order to overcome the limitations they face as individual human beings. Despite the theological and philosophical differences that divide them, Koreans are united by this Korean approach to spirituality.

CHAPTER 7

The Spiritual Practices of Koreans

Given the great variety of gods and other potential foci of a spiritual gaze available to Koreans, it is not surprising that there is also a rich assortment of spiritual practices available for them to choose from. Koreans can pray loudly or silently, alone or in groups, and they can meditate quietly, again alone or in groups. While some may choose to sing sacred songs in praise of their God, others may prefer to dance to entertain various spirits. Some engage in spiritual practices in order to discipline themselves against the temptations of this material world, while others engage in religious ritual in the hope it will gain them material benefits.

Some spiritual practices are designed primarily to help practitioners personally experience the presence of something greater than themselves, though what that something is can vary from a supernatural personality to an impersonal cosmic force. Other spiritual activities are seen as a way for supplicants to gain the assistance of some powerful supernatural personality in solving some immediate financial or health problem. There are also religious rituals that are primarily displays of worship of and devotion to a powerful, benevolent deity. Still another reason some Koreans devote time and energy to spiritual activities is to advance themselves toward the long-term goal of personal salvation, though how that salvation is defined can vary from eternal life in paradise after death to an escape from the cycle of birth-death-rebirth.

There are also some who devote time and energy to spiritual practices out of more altruistic motives. Some pray or participate in religious exercises in the belief that by doing so they will bring salvation to others. They may hope to hasten the creation of a paradise in which men and women can live without fear of disease, poverty, or injustice, or they may think that their actions will speed the progress of a recently dead loved one to a better form of existence in their next reincarnation. Some spiritual practices and rituals are intended to strengthen group solidarity, such as in a family whose members travel from near and far to honor a parent or grandparent in an ancestor memorial service or in a village whose residents pray together to thank the tutelary deity of their village for protection provided over the past year. And sometimes people engage in ritual and other spiritual practices because it feels good. Some spiritual practices, such as cinnabar-field breathing, are believed to enhance the health and longevity of those who engage in them or at the very least to promote peace of mind. Some rituals attract participants simply because they are familiar and enjoyable.

A familiar ritual can be very comforting. It can allow participants to escape from the anxiety of confronting a new situation and not knowing what to do, because, by its very definition, a familiar ritual is one they have performed or witnessed before. That is one reason a regular weekly worship service can be a welcome escape from a stressful workplace. In addition, a familiar ritual may stimulate pleasant memories of a time when the observer or participant performed or witnessed that same ritual. Rituals can also help participants overcome a recent traumatic or unpleasant experience by allowing them to return to the familiar and comfortable, or by turning their attention from whatever unpleasant experience they endured and putting them in another frame of mind. Funerals, for example, can direct our attention away from the loss of a loved one and toward thoughts of the better state of existence that the loved one now enjoys. Finally, Koreans, like people elsewhere, may participate in a ritual or engage in a spiritual practice as a way of gaining prestige. Playing a leading role in a community ritual can enhance the celebrant's social status, as can successfully completing a spiritual exercise that others found too daunting, such as a marathon meditation session.

Most people engage in spiritual practices for a mixture of reasons. Take pilgrimage, for example. Pilgrims may join a group tour to sacred sites because they expect to enjoy both the scenery and the camaraderie that comes from traveling with a like-minded group.

However, they may also hope to gain some spiritual merit from their visit to those sacred sites, and they may believe that what they will see and learn at those sites will strengthen their faith and give them both the will and the way to become better human beings. In addition, they may plan on praying for help in solving some pressing problem, assuming that prayer at a sacred site is more likely to be heard than a prayer said in the privacy of the home.

Not all spiritual practices are rituals, if by "ritual" we mean a series of actions or words that are sanctified by their predictability and consistency as well as by their spiritual import. Understood as such, rituals are spiritual practices that follow a script to ensure that their content does not significantly vary with differences in time, place, or performer; but some spiritual practices are more spontaneous and informal. The Korean who adds a pebble to the top of a pile of pebbles along the path to a mountainside Buddhist temple is not enacting a formal ritual. He or she is simply making a prayer to the mountain god that protects travelers on that trail. Alternatively, he or she may be simply imitating what those ahead of them on that trail did.

It is important to keep in mind that when you watch Koreans perform a ritual or engage in some other spiritual practice, you cannot necessarily infer from their actions a belief in supernatural beings or even a belief in the efficacy of that ritual. Christian missionaries in Korea made that mistake in the nineteenth century when they assumed that everyone who bowed toward an ancestral spirit tablet during a Confucian ancestor memorial service believed that the ancestors actually dwelled in that tablet and could enjoy the food offered to them during that service. Though some who performed that universal ritual probably believed the spirits of their ancestors were actually present before them, others understood that ritual to be merely an expression of respectful remembrance by the participants.

Koreans may engage in a spiritual practice in a "just in case" frame of mind, under the assumption that such actions cannot do any harm, and they may help, so why not do them? At the very least, performing a ritual or engaging in some other spiritual practice can make participants feel that they are either doing something that might resolve a problem that afflicts them, or that they are playing their proper roles in their family or community and are therefore contributing to harmony and solidarity among family, neighbors, and friends.

Anthropocentric Spiritual Practices

One reason for the great variety of spiritual practices in Korea is that Koreans do not necessarily pay much attention to the boundaries between religious traditions that scholars often emphasize. We saw in chapter 6 that there is no strict one-to-one correlation between one Korean ethical principle and one Korean religious tradition. Many different religious and spiritual traditions share many of the same ethical principles in Korea. The same is true of spiritual practices. Koreans from many different theological perspectives adopt similar spiritual practices. Moreover, people within the same spiritual tradition draw upon a wide range of spiritual practices to achieve their spiritual goals.

For example, Buddhists meditate, but they are not the only ones who do so. During the Chosŏn dynasty, Neo-Confucians meditated, and in the modern era, not only Won Buddhists but also followers of some of the other new religions meditate. Catholics, too, can be said to meditate, though their approach to meditation is usually more theocentric than anthropocentric. Catholics and other Christians are better known for their theocentric prayers, but Buddhists also pray. Korean participants in anthropocentric traditions sometimes engage in theocentric practices, just as those in theocentric traditions sometimes engage in anthropocentric practices.

An anthropocentric spiritual practice, like an anthropocentric spiritual gaze, focuses on this world, on human nature, human emotions, the individual human body, and the groups to which the practitioner belongs, rather than outward toward a supernatural personality. Anthropocentric spiritual practices typically are a form of self-cultivation intended to help the practitioner discover and activate his or her true self. Sometimes that true inner nature is defined as being identical with the true nature of the cosmos, in which case the practitioner strives to became one with the universe, blurring the boundary between inner-directed and outer-directed spirituality.

The most typical form of anthropocentric spiritual practice is, of course, meditation. There are many kinds of meditation practiced in Korea. The best known in the West is the sitting mediation of Korea's Buddhist monks. Younger monks engage in meditation in groups in their monastery's meditation hall, and senior monks may retreat from the others in the meditation hall to meditate alone in a hermitage farther up the mountain. Whether done in a group or alone, monastic meditation in Korea has the goal of calming the mind so that the distractions and emotions that keep it from perceiving its own true nature are eliminated. One way to do that is to try to shut down the mind, emptying it of all thoughts. Philosophical Buddhism teaches that the silent mind is the true mind, the inner Buddha nature.

However, Buddhism also recognizes that it is not easy to simply empty our minds. Therefore, it teaches us to pay attention to the role our human minds play in creating the very distractions that keep us from perceiving our true nature. As one noted Buddhist scholar explains, by "tracing back the radiance"—focusing our attention not on the world outside but on the mind that creates that world—we can eventually gain insight into the transitory, dependent, and therefore unreliable nature of all phenomena. Such insight constitutes enlightenment. When we are enlightened to the true nature of the world created by our minds, we become enlightened to the true nature of our own minds. We recognize and thus become at one with our own true Buddha nature.

Another way Buddhist meditators try to shut down the misleading activity of their minds is to force the mind to recognize its own limitations. Our minds introduce distinctions into the phenomenal world that mask the undifferentiated nature of thusness. Therefore, we need to teach our minds that analytical thinking is not 100 percent reliable. We can do that by focusing on a "critical phrase" (what Koreans call a "hwadu") in a statement or conversation that cannot be understood through the analytical tools of logical thinking. For example, Buddhist meditators have focused on the answer a Chinese monk gave long ago when he was asked if a dog had a Buddha nature. The answer was, "Mu," which can mean either "no" or "it is empty" (which is essentially the same thing as Buddha nature). Can both meanings be correct? That is the logical conundrum that teaches us

Lay Buddhists engaged in group meditation. Photo courtesy of Neungin Sunwon Buddhist center in southern Seoul.

that the fit between language (and the analytical thinking that makes language possible) and reality is not perfect; therefore, we cannot rely on language and analytical thinking alone for insight into the fundamental nature of reality.

Not all who meditate in Korea do so in order to empty their minds. Some instead strive to cultivate an attitude of mindfulness, of focused attention on the world around them and on their reactions to it so that they will always react appropriately. That was the aim of Neo-Confucian meditation, and it is the aim of Won Buddhists today.

Neo-Confucians denigrated Buddhists for focusing their attention on nothingness. When Neo-Confucians engaged in "quiet sitting" (the term for their form of meditation), they focused on the underlying unity of the cosmos created by the cosmic network of appropriate interactions. When they sat quietly for hours at a time and focused their attention on that cosmic network, they weren't looking at the phenomenal world as unreal. Instead, they were trying to understand the interconnected patterns of that world better so they could act in accordance with them. The goal of Neo-Confucian meditation was to gain a clear vision of those patterns so they could remain mindful of them as they went about their daily lives.

Though Neo-Confucianism has faded into institutional invisibility in Korea today, Won Buddhism is a visible presence on the modern Korean religious landscape. Won Buddhism is known in Korea for replacing a focus on sitting mediation with what Won Buddhists call "timeless zen and placeless zen." By zen, in that context, Won Buddhism means maintaining a focused mind (what they call "mindfulness"), in which we remain aware at all times of our fourfold debt of gratitude to our parents, our fellow human beings, our natural environment, and the laws that give stability to society. However, Won Buddhists recognize that in order to maintain such a focus amid all the distractions of everyday life, we need to clear our minds of any ideas or fleeting thoughts that weaken that focus. Therefore, Won Buddhism also suggests a couple of other spiritual practices that are believed to clear the mind of all but the most appropriate thoughts and help us cultivate the virtue that is our true human nature

One practice Won Buddhism suggests is sitting meditation, much like what Buddhist monks engage in. Just like mainstream Buddhists, they suggest that those engaged in sitting meditation assume the lotus position, with their legs intertwined. They also suggest that, while sitting with their legs crossed, meditators concentrate their physical energy and mental attention on the *tanjŏn* ("cinnabar field"), the invisible spot below the navel in the lower abdomen that is believed by many Koreans to be the center of energy in the body. At the same time, they should control their breathing so that it is slow and regular. Correct posture, proper breathing, and concentrated attention on the *tanjŏn* will clear the mind of the self-centered thoughts and delusions that Won Buddhists want to eliminate.

For some, however, just sitting and breathing is not enough to stop the flow of distracting and inappropriate thoughts. For such people, Won Buddhism advises chanting the Buddha's name over and over again. The chant it suggests is a standard Buddhist chant, "all hail the Amitabha Buddha," though Won Buddhist meditation guidelines say that chanters should keep in mind that Buddha is not a supernatural being out there somewhere in the universe but instead is the Buddha nature that is our own true mind.

Neither mediation nor chanting is a regular part of Won Buddhist Sunday services. Sunday services look a lot like Protestant Christian services, with prayers, hymns, reading from the scriptures, and a sermon, but no time set aside for group mediation. Moreover, those Sunday services are better attended than the early-morning weekday meditation sessions at the Won Buddhist temples I visited. Won Buddhism is predominantly an urban religion, and few city dwellers can find the time to sit and meditate on a regular basis.

Won Buddhists are not the only Koreans who focus on their cinnabar field when they find the time to meditate. Nor are they the only Koreans who chant. Focusing attention on the cinnabar field and on regulating breathing while meditating, as Won Buddhists are told to do, is popular these days with followers of at least one other new religion, as well as with members of an organization that says it is spiritual but not religious. The new religion that encourages cinnabar-field meditation has no relationship to Buddhism. Taejonggyo, as we saw in chapter 6, worships Tan'gun, the god-man whom the followers of Taejonggyo believe was the first king in Korea and the founder of the Korean race. Taejonggyo's adherents also believe that Tan'gun created the technique of cinnabar-field breathing to help his descendants remain spiritually and physically strong. (Though cinnabar-field breathing has been part of the internal alchemy practices of Chinese Daoism for well over a thousand years, Taejonggyo insists that Chinese Daoists learned that technique from ancient Koreans.)

This Taejonggyo belief has been promoted by Dahn World, along with some recently "rediscovered" texts that both Taejonggyo and Dahn World believe to date to almost three thousand years ago, to the time of Tan'gun, providing the textual basis for cinnabar-field breathing. However, Dahn World, as noted in chapter 5, insists it is not a religion, because it does not preach belief in any God or gods. Instead, it teaches that through the regular practice of cinnabar-field meditation, accompanied by specific stretching exercises it has developed, practitioners can replace the weakened life-sustaining energy *(ki)* in their bodies with fresh, strong energy from the cosmos. Not only will this make practitioners stronger and healthier; they will also find that absorbing cosmic energy makes them one with the universe. According to Dahn World, if only 100 million people engage in the Dahn World techniques of cinnabar-field meditation (which it now calls "brain respiration"), they will form a critical mass with enough vitalized cosmic energy to inspire an "enlightenment revolution" all over the world.

Dahn World is evidence that meditation is not confined to organizations that define themselves as religious. Another spiritual (but not religious) organization that preaches the need for and benefits of meditation goes by the name of Maum Meditation Center. ("Maum" is the Korean word for the heart-and-mind that controls our thoughts and emotions.) Though Maum Meditation was not founded until 1996, it has now expanded beyond Korea and operates centers in North and South America, Japan, Europe, and Australia. At those centers, you will see no religious images or sacred texts. Instead, you will find instructors eager to teach you how to empty your mind. Rather than asking meditators to focus their attention on their cinnabar field and on their breathing, Maum Meditation instructors guide practitioners in clearing their minds of all thoughts and memories that mislead them into thinking of themselves as separate and distinct individuals. According to Maum Meditation, once meditators clear their minds, they will discover their true selves, which are one with the universe.

Though various forms of anthropocentric meditation can be found both inside and outside religious organizations, chanting as a meditative strategy is normally an indication that the chanter is a member of a religious organization and is not just practicing private spirituality. We already saw that Won Buddhists sometimes chant as an aid to meditation. Mainstream Buddhists also chant. In fact, monks are supposed to wake up around three in the morning so they can go to the main ritual hall and engage in choral chanting of sutras and other Buddhist texts to the beat of a wooden gong. This early-morning chanting is not so much a form of meditation, however, as it is a mental discipline preparing monks to meditate later that morning or at least to put them in a mindful state of awareness as they go through the tasks of the day ahead.

The new religion Ch'ŏndogyo also promotes chanting that is not meditation per se. In fact, in Ch'ŏndogyo, chanting is not even an aid to meditation. Instead, it is used in place of quiet meditation. Ch'ŏndogyo members are told to repeatedly chant the twenty-one-syllable mantra (discussed in chapters 5 and 6) that calls for the animating energy of the cosmos to descend upon them and make its presence felt as God within. Ch'ŏndogyo practitioners are less interested in clearing their minds of self-centered thoughts than in experiencing the presence of the divine. They chant their mantra with the help of a rosary that has either 21 or 105 beads (for chanting the incantation 5 times). Chanting is the most important spiritual practice for Ch'ŏndogyo believers. They chant that mantra as part of their Sunday worship services, and they chant it in the short ritual that Ch'ŏndogyo families engage in at home at 9 p.m. every evening. Ch'ŏndogyo believers can also chant on retreats in which they engage in chanting almost as intensively as monks in marathon mediation sessions engage in meditation.

The Chŭngsan family of religions, including Daesun Jinri-hoe and Jeungsan-do, also stress chanting, but they have their own set of incantations. The most popular is called the T'aeul chant because it begins with the line, *"Humch'i, humch'i, T'aeul ch'ŏnsang won'gun."* Those sounds have no meaning in themselves, but they are said to reproduce the cosmic breathing of heaven and earth. The T'aeul chant is said to have the power to heal an ill chanter and to bring chanters peace of mind. What is more important, it is believed to hasten the day when the Great Transformation will replace the earth of today with a paradise in which disease and injustice have been eliminated.

Chŭngsan believers chant incantations in rituals at worship halls, and they are also supposed to chant incantations twice a day at home on days they don't go to a worship hall. Chanting in the Chŭngsan family of religions straddles the fence between anthropocentric and theocentric spiritual practices. On the one hand, the incantation is supposed to be so powerful that simply chanting it properly will bring about the desired effects. On the other hand, many of their chants can also be interpreted as praise for their God Kang Chŭngsan, who promoted the use of that chant; such chants could thus be considered a form of theocentric prayer.

Catholic chanting, when saying the rosary, can also be said to be open to interpretation in two different ways. When Catholics hold their rosary and repeat aloud the "Our Father" and the "Hail Mary" prayers over and over again, they are told to focus their thoughts on the passion of Christ or other events in the life of Christ and his mother Mary while they are chanting those prayers. Saying the rosary, therefore, is a form of meditation, though it is not the sort of anthropocentric meditation that looks inward to human nature. Instead, Catholic rosary meditation is theocentric, focusing on Jesus Christ, whom Christians believe is God incarnate in human flesh. As such, the Catholic rosary can also be interpreted as a form of prayer, either of praise for God or as a way of asking God or Mary, the mother of Jesus, to answer a burning question or solve a problem that otherwise looks unsolvable.

Theocentric Religious Practices

Prayer is, by definition, theocentric. You don't pray to yourself. Instead you pray to a superior being. Prayer can be either a request for assistance or a display of devotion. Either way, prayer necessarily involves a relationship between the person praying and the being prayed to. However, the manner in which prayer is used to address and interact with a supernatural being varies greatly across the wide range of practices that comprise Korean spirituality. Prayer can be sedate and solemn, or it can emotional and loud. Prayer can be done primarily with words, or it can require material offerings. Koreans may pray with no expectation of an immediate response, or they may expect their prayers to result in a personal encounter with the divine.

The most emotional and loudest approaches to praying are found in two very different religious traditions, shamanism and Protestant Christianity. Shaman rituals are not usually described as a form of prayer, but that is what they are, if we define prayer as directing words and gifts toward a supernatural being. In a shaman ritual, a shaman prays to spirits on behalf of her clients. In a full-scale ritual, she will interact with a number of different spirits, ranging from recently deceased relatives of the clients who commissioned that ritual to powerful spirit generals. She doesn't always treat those spirits with the dignity other religious traditions accord their deities. If she wants those spirits to do something for her client, she may argue with them, bribe them, entertain them, or even order them around.

A shaman ritual *(kut)* has three main stages: the invocation of the spirits, the entertaining of and asking favors of the spirits, and the sending off of the spirits. However, those rituals are never the same twice (except in the case of rituals that have been named national cultural treasures and have to follow the script that was given that appellation). A good shaman is one who tailors her ritual to the needs and expectations of the individual or the family that commissioned the ritual.

A shaman ritual might involve divinatory actions, such as count-ing rice grains that have been thrown up in the air up by the shaman (if the number of rice grains the shaman catches is an even num-ber, that is a sign that good luck is coming). Shaman rituals also of-ten involve offerings of food and money (the shaman accepts money on behalf of the spirits). However, it is the music and the costumes that keep a shaman ritual from being too solemn. Shamans are often accompanied by musicians who bang on percussion instruments or blow wind instruments. The music is loud and fast, because it is de-signed to win the attention of the spirits, and the music is often ac-companied by the dancing of the shaman. The costumes a shaman wears, particularly those worn by a charismatic shaman, are also at-tention-getting. If she is possessed by a powerful spirit, she may wear a premodern military or civilian official costume. However, if she is channeling someone who has recently died, she may also dress in clothes that resemble those that spirit wore when it inhabited a hu-man body. Sometimes shamans dress in what is described as Bud-dhist monks' clothing, with Buddhist headgear (a white hood), but such clothing is unlike any Buddhist costume I have ever seen. At other times, a shaman may wear the shaman version of a traditional official's stovepipe hat. Even though she may wear male clothing on the upper part of her body and her head, she normally wears female clothing from the waist down. (Even the rare male shaman wears a skirt under his costumes when he performs a ritual.)

Not all folk religion practices are noisy and complicated. A household ritual known as a *kosa* can be very short and simple. A *kosa* is a rite of thanksgiving performed by the female head of a household, thanking the various household gods for all they have done for the family in the past and asking them to continue such good work in the future. (These days, a *kosa* can also be performed by shamans at the opening of a new business to ask the gods to help that business prosper.) A *kosa* involves no loud music, costume changes, dancing, or arguing with the gods. Instead, a *kosa* consists of a few short words plus offerings of food and drink. A *kosa* is so short and simple that it seems inappropriate to call it worship of the gods, just as the informal language, folk dancing, and loud music of a shaman ritual also seems to defy labeling as worship. Instead, they both should be best seen as forms of prayer, supplications to supernatural beings.

Christians praying in a church, though their prayers can be as noisy and informal as prayers in shaman rituals, would not be at all displeased to hear their words and actions described as worship. Sometimes all they are doing is praising God, in which case the label "worship" is completely appropriate. At other times, though, they are asking God for help with a specific problem or just for general assistance in gaining health and wealth. Whether they are worshipping or supplicating, Korean Protestant Christians display an emotional exuberance rarely seen in Korea before Christianity arrived, except in shaman rituals. However, unlike the folk religion, Christianity is doctrine-oriented. That gives it an intellectual rigor traditional Korea associated with monastic Buddhism and Neo-Confucianism. Combining aspects of both sides of Korea's traditional spiritual culture —the enthusiasm of the folk religion and the scholarship of the traditions imported from China—Christianity then added a new element to Korean spirituality: lay participation. Despite the informality of a shaman ritual, most of the dancing, singing, and talking in that ritual is done by the shaman. Members of the audience may occasionally engage in verbal exchanges with the shaman, but for the most part they are spectators rather than participants. The same can be said of monastic Buddhist rituals: lay visitors to a monastery did not normally join in the chanting of the monks. In Christian churches, however, the pastor operates somewhat like a cheerleader. His congregation sings hymns loudly and joyfully, shouts out amens and hallelujahs, and raises its arms high to receive the Holy Spirit.

Many Korean Protestant churches represent the sort of experiential Christianity that is often associated with Pentecostal Christianity in North America. Most Korean Christians believe that an intellectual acceptance of the Christian message is not enough for salvation. Instead, they insist that those who have not felt God's saving grace in their heart cannot be assured of salvation. Just as Buddhists need to have the emotional experience of enlightenment to feel truly enlightened, so too do Christians need to have the emotional experience of being born again to be truly saved.

In many of Korea's churches, Christianity is not just experiential; it is also very practical, concerned not only with salvation after death but also with basking in God's love before death. The largest church in the world, Seoul's Yoido Full Gospel Holiness Church, has attracted hundreds of thousands of members by preaching that those who truly love God will not only be granted eternal happiness in heaven after death; God will also grant them both health and wealth in this life. In other words, the truly godly will be blessed not just spiritually but also financially and physically.

This practical bent of Korean Protestant Christianity is particularly obvious in the many "prayer mountains" (retreat centers) that have sprung up all over Korea. These retreat centers are usually built in the same sorts of quiet mountain settings that shamans and Buddhist monks preferred. Koreans flock to those retreat centers to engage in intense prayer and worship sessions, often accompanied by fasting, in the hope that God will be so impressed by their display of devotion that he will solve whatever spiritual, physical, or financial problem is bothering them. Such centers often advertise that miracles occur on their premises regularly, and they even cite testimonials in those ads from worshippers who say they were suffering from an incurable disease until they visited that particular retreat center. Those who can't take enough time away from their family or their work to spend a few days in a rural retreat center can hope for the same benefits by attending the dawn prayer meetings or late-night Friday prayer meetings offered by many urban Protestant churches. It is not unusual for a Korean businessman to attend a 5 a.m. weekday service before he goes to his office or for the members of a congregation to drop by their church late on a Friday evening and stay there until 2 or 3 a.m., singing hymns, engaging in choral reading of the scriptures, praying aloud, and listening to a short sermon.

Catholic churches are somewhat more sedate (though Korean Catholics enjoy singing hymns as much as Protestants do). However, Korean Catholics tend to stay at church longer on Sundays than North American Catholics usually do, arriving early and leaving quite a while after mass ends. The Catholic Church in Korea has adopted the Korean Protestant practice of dividing congregations into small cell-groups of about ten members who live relatively close to each other. Those cell-groups meet on weekday evenings for communal prayer and Bible study.

Buddhists also pray, of course, though the way lay Buddhists approach prayer is quite different from prayer in shaman rituals or Christian services. One popular method of Buddhist prayer is to repeatedly bow before a statue or painting of a buddha or bodhisattva, bending at the waist and bending your knees so that your knees and head touch the floor, while saying over and over again the name of the particular Buddhist deity you are asking for help. Sometimes Buddhists will perform 108 such prostrations in a row to remind themselves to beware of the 108 different causes of human suffering.

Some temples are known as particularly efficacious places to pray to particular buddhas or bodhisattvas or to make specific requests. The hermitage near the summit of Mt. Kwanak-san, near Seoul National University, for instance, is said to be a good place to pray for success in university entrance examinations. For someone who is ill, a good place to go to be cured is Mt. P'algong-san near the city of Taegu, where you can pray to statues of the Healing Buddha. And those who want to pray to the bodhisattva of compassion go to the Pori-am hermitage high up on a cliff on Korea's southeastern coast.

Followers of Korea's new religions pray as well. Most of them (with the conspicuous exceptions of the Chŭngsan religions) have adopted the Christian practice of holding regular Sunday worship services for believers to engage in communal prayers, the singing of hymns, and the reading of scriptures. The officiants at such services usually give a sermon as well. Won Buddhist, Ch'ŏndogyo, and Taejonggyo services resemble services at Korean Protestant Churches, except that the scriptures that are read, the hymns that are sung, and the objects of the prayers that are said are quite different, and the congregation isn't usually nearly as exuberant.

In congregational Taejonggyo services, for example, worshippers burn incense, bow toward an altar, chant a sacred mantra, pray, sing hymns, chant scriptures, and listen to sermons. Their actions are not much different from what would be seen at a subdued Christian service. However, unlike Christians, some followers of Korea's new religions also have altars at home for family rituals on days when they don't go to an official worship hall. For example, Ch'ŏndogyo believers are supposed to maintain altars in their homes on which they place a bowl of clean, pure water at 9 p.m., as a reminder of the pure hearts of the founders of Ch'ŏndogyo. The whole family should be present for this ritual. After the bowl of clean water has been offered up, they are all supposed to chant the twenty-one-syllable incantation five times in unison.

Members of the Unification Church, the only major new religion that originated from within Christianity, also maintain altars in their homes for family rituals. Their church tells its members to erect those altars in a room designated for use as a family prayer room. The altars are supposed to hold pictures of the True Parents (Sun Myung Moon and his wife). There should also be a container of the Holy Salt believed to repel evil spirits. On Unification Church Holy Days, offerings of fruit, nuts, and candles are added to the altars.

Group-Oriented Spiritual Practices

Koreans also engage in spiritual practices that may contain elements of prayer or meditation but take as their primary focus human beings with whom the practitioner interacts on a regular basis. The horizontal spiritual gaze seen in group-oriented spiritual practices, with roots in Confucianism, is nonetheless a spiritual gaze because the purpose of such practices is to overcome the limitations of existence as a separate and distinct individual by joining forces with others, and because these practices involve supernatural beings or forces.

A good example of a group-oriented spiritual practice would be ancestor memorial services. Misunderstood as "ancestor worship" by early Christian missionaries in Korea, the ancestor memorial service is a manifestation of the love and respect Koreans hold for parents, grandparents, and other ancestors. On the anniversary of the death of a beloved parent or grandparent, as well as on important holidays such as the Autumn Harvest Festival and Lunar New Year, family members will meet to join in the ritual display of filial piety known in Korean as *"chesa."* If they follow the traditional Confucian practice, they will offer food and drink to the spirits of the ancestors. The men in the family will also prostrate themselves before the grave or, if the ritual is held at home, before a spirit tablet (a piece of paper on which the name of the deceased is written). Traditionally, the women in the family participated by preparing the food that the men offer. However, some Korean families have recently begun allowing daughters to show their filial love by joining the men in making food offerings and bowing before the spirit tablet. Even in the most modern families, the standard practice is still to have the eldest son in the direct line of patrilineal descent lead the bowing.

Families that follow the Confucian tradition of honoring ancestors know that there is a right way and a wrong way to arrange the food placed on the offering table. Red-colored fruits should be placed to the east, while pale-colored fruits belong in the west. Fish should be in the east (with its tail pointing to the west), and meat should be in the west. Christianity and some of the new religions, modifying Confucian ritual procedures, have created new ancestor memorial rituals that allow them to honor deceased parents and grandparents in a way they feel is more appropriate. For example, Christians do not offer food to the ancestors or bow before a spirit tablet. Instead, family members join in prayers and the singing of hymns in homage to a departed loved one.

Korean Christians created their own ancestor memorial ritual because, on the one hand, church leaders told them that bowing before a spirit tablet was a form of idolatry; but on the other hand they did not want to appear unfilial. After all, for centuries Koreans had believed that a person could not be considered moral if he did not display proper love and respect for his parents and grandparents. Rather than challenging that traditional Korean value, Korean Christians have embraced it. Not only have they developed a Christianized ancestral memorial ritual; one church, the Full Gospel Church in the city of Inch'ŏn, has opened a Graduate School of Filial Piety.

When family members come together to display through ritual their love and affection for their ancestors, they do more than just show that they are filial descendants. They also affirm their identity as a family. Rituals performed collectively reinforce emotional bonds joining the various participants to one another, giving them a collective strength they would not have as solitary individuals. We see the same benefit of congregational solidarity in much larger Confucian rituals, one performed twice a year at the National Confucian Shrine in Seoul and another performed at the shrine to the spirits of the kings and queens of the Chosŏn dynasty. In these slow, solemn rituals, men dressed in traditional robes offer food and drink to the enshrined spirits. In between offerings, they move in unison in a sort of ritual dance, though they move so slowly that it does not look much like what we ordinarily think of as a dance. Those rituals are seen now as more cultural than religious in nature; accordingly, they have been designated as national cultural treasures. For observers, the slow movement of dancers in colorful costumes provides a pleasing aesthetic experience. However, the participants often find those rituals a spiritual experience, filling them with the emotional realization that they are not alone in the world but instead are linked to the generations that preceded them. Whether or not they believe spirits actually dwell in those shrines is less important than the feeling of solidarity the ritual inspires.

Rituals to honor the dead are not the only group-oriented spiritual practices Koreans engage in. As we saw in chapter 2, premodern Koreans living in the same village would join together once a year in village rites thanking the tutelary deities of that village for the protection provided over the previous year and asking them to continue providing protection in the year ahead. Some villages held Confucian rites, with the senior men in the village serving as officiants. Others would call in a shaman to lead them in a less sedate display of gratitude to the guardian gods of that village. Still other villages would combine the two, restraining any untoward displays of emotion during a Confucian ritual of thanksgiving but then letting their hair down afterward and dancing to fast-paced folk music to show their guardian deities how pleased they were with their protection. Whatever form a village ritual took, it reinforced feelings of solidarity among the villagers, reminding them that they were not alone and could count on the help of not only the tutelary deities but their human neighbors as well.

Those few village rites that survive today function more as displays of pride in traditional culture than as actual expressions of gratitude to village gods. Nevertheless, they still represent Korean spirituality in practice, to the extent that through these rituals, participants overcome the limitations of existence as individuals by linking with a powerful invisible presence, in this case a close-knit community that embraces both past and present generations and includes the village gods. The spiritual significance of these kinds of rituals can be seen in other group-oriented spiritual practices that are thriving in contemporary Korea, such as weddings.

In traditional Korea, Buddhist monks did not officiate at weddings, nor would a shaman be asked to play an important role in a wedding (except in the rare case of a ghost marriage between a man and woman who had died single though of marriageable age). Traditional wedding rituals normally followed a format provided in Confucian ritual guidebooks and made no reference to gods or other supernatural forces. The focus was on the families of the bride and the groom, because in traditional Korea a marriage was more of a joining of two families than it was a joining of two individuals.

Most weddings in Korea today no longer follow the traditional format. The most popular site for a wedding in the twenty-first century is a secular wedding hall (which may look like a small castle or a department store from the outside), not a church or a temple. Christianity introduced Koreans to the notion of a marriage ritual in which a couple swear their love for each other before God and their community, thereby sanctifying their relationship. That notion has now spread to several of Korea's new religions, and they have created their own marriage rituals. Such wedding ceremonies, however, retain the traditional group orientation, in that the bride and groom do not swear their love for each other in private. Instead, a wedding ceremony is a public commitment—made not only before God but also before friends and relatives—that the new couple will form a stable social unit that will contribute to society.

This public orientation of a wedding ceremony is especially obvious in the mass weddings held by the Unification Church, which they call "The Blessing," in which Sun Myung Moon joins hundreds or sometimes even thousands of couples in sacred matrimony at one time. Even the marriage of just one man and one woman before a few friends and relatives is a public event. The presence of other people witnessing the very personal expression of two people's undying love for each other gives the new couple hope that, with the support of all those friends and relatives, they will be able to honor the commitment they have just made to each other. Married through a religious ritual in front of people who share their spiritual orientation, the happy couple often finds that such a public ceremony increases their confidence in their ability to remain in love despite all the challenges that living together and raising a family may throw their way.

Funerals are another group-oriented spiritual practice. When a loved one dies, those left behind do not want to be alone. They need to draw on the strength they can receive from friends and relatives. Moreover, a funeral ritual performed in the presence of others who also knew the person being mourned helps mourners accept the finality of death, because such an unpleasant fact is easier to accept when we can see that others we know and trust have accepted it as well. There is a wide variety of funeral rituals in Korea, ranging from a Christian service in which the soul is commended to God, to Buddhist services over the forty-nine days after death to pray that the loved one will be reborn in a higher level of existence. (Secular funerals are also available for the 47 percent of the Korean population that has no religious affiliation.) Whatever the particular form a religious grieving ritual takes, in addition to calling on supernatural assistance at this time of great personal distress, funerals provide the comfort of enhanced group solidarity, as the recognition of shared loss brings participants in the ritual closer together. Moreover, funerals with a spiritual component comfort the bereaved with answers to questions about what happened to the person mourned after her body died. Such answers become more believable, and therefore more comforting, when they are also accepted by those accompanying the mourner at the funeral.

A more pleasant form of group-oriented spiritual practice is the pilgrimage. In premodern Korea, individuals would occasionally travel on foot to a famous temple or other sacred site in search of supernatural assistance or spiritual consolation. However, in the latter half of the twentieth century, group pilgrimages grew in popularity. The first significant group pilgrimages were organized by the Catholic Church, which dispatches buses full of parishioners to sites sanctified by the blood of martyrs. The Catholic Church has built large churches on many of those sacred sites, as well as educational markers explaining what happened at those locations during the persecutions of the eighteenth and nineteenth centuries. Catholics go on those pilgrimages to pray and to learn more about the history of Korean Catholicism. However, by traveling in groups of like-minded believers, they also strengthen their faith. Finding themselves in the company of people who share their beliefs, they become even more firmly convinced that their beliefs are correct and even more determined to act in accordance with those beliefs. Pilgrimages create congregational solidarity, which strengthens individual determination.

Other religious communities in Korea have imitated the Catholic example. Won Buddhism invites pilgrims to the places where its founder first preached and established the first Won Buddhist institutions. Ch'ŏndogyo has built a retreat house for communal chanting near the sacred spot where its founder had his first revelations. Even mainstream Buddhist monks have begun advertising pilgrimage tours, in which they lead groups of lay Buddhists to various important temples on the Korean peninsula. No matter which religious organization organizes a pilgrimage, the reasons are the same: a pilgrimage not only gives believers a chance to pray or meditate, something they could do more easily at home or in their local ritual center; it also allows them to overcome the loneliness of existence as a separate and distinct individual by acting in concert with others who have the same beliefs and the same spiritual practices.

The discussion above of anthropocentric, theocentric, and group-oriented spiritual practices does not exhaust the types of spiritual practices available to Koreans. There are also rituals of repentance, such as the Catholic sacrament of confession, in which sinners confess their sins to a priest and, if they are truly contrite, have their sins forgiven. Another ritual of repentance is the monastic Buddhist practice of recalling one's mistakes, not in order to seek forgiveness but in order to remind oneself not to make such mistakes again. There are also rituals of salvation, such as the Christian rite of baptism, which is believed to give an individual believer a fresh start on the road to salvation, and the Daesun Jinri-hoe ritual of cosmic renewal, which is performed to hasten the Great Transformation that will end the troubles that plague humanity in this world and create a paradise on earth.

One spiritual practice growing in popularity in Korea is the study of sacred writings. The spread of Bible-study groups that has accompanied the rise of Christianity has stimulated the formation of sutra-study groups among well-educated lay Buddhists, as well as a focus among followers of the various new religions on their own sacred writings. Another spiritual practice that has become prominent recently—though it has been part of Korean spirituality since the arrival of Buddhist missionaries sixteen hundred years ago—is proselytizing, the act of trying to convince others to share your beliefs and adopt your spiritual practices so that they, too, can be saved. Christian missionaries revitalized the practice of proselytizing in Korea; as a result, Christians have been the most ardent proselytizers for the past century or so. That is one reason Christianity has grown so fast in Korea.

However, other communities have begun to respond with proselytizing of their own. I've seen Buddhists distributing religious literature on the streets of Seoul, and I've seen advertisements for organizations such as Dahn World plastered on the walls of subway stations. Daesun Jinri-hoe is known for encouraging followers to approach strangers on the street and ask them, "Do you know what the

True Way is?" Won Buddhism, on the other hand, proselytizes by example. Won Buddhists engage in charitable work around the world, both out of a desire to act in accordance with the Buddhist virtue of compassion but also in the hope that others will be drawn to Won Buddhist teachings by the model of practical spirituality Won Buddhists provide.

The range of Korean spiritual practices is so broad that almost anyone, whether they believe in one God, many gods, or no gods, can find a spiritual practice they feel comfortable with and a community of fellow practitioners ready to welcome them. Whether they are interested in cultivating their innate potential for becoming one with the cosmos, or in soliciting assistance from God in dealing with a financial or health problem; whether they want to improve their chances for going to paradise after they die or they want to create a paradise on earth; Koreans can find like-minded individuals to work with to achieve their goals. Contemporary Korea offers individuals a vast array of goals and techniques to choose from when they embark on a spiritual quest. Nevertheless, whichever approach to spirituality they prefer, it is likely to be a Korean approach, emphasizing the traditional Korean desire to overcome the limitations of existence as a separate and distinct individual and providing spiritual techniques for doing just that.

Spirituality in North Korea

Korea was one country with one culture for most of the last thousand years. However, the struggle beginning in 1945 between the United States and the Soviet Union for influence in East Asia led to the division of Korea into what became two radically different societies. In the preceding chapters, all discussion of modern (post-1945) Korean spirituality has concerned the Republic of Korea (South Korea). There are two reasons for this focus on the southern half of the peninsula. First, it is difficult to gain much meaningful information about religious beliefs and practices in North Korea, in contrast to the abundance of information available in the open society of South Korea. Also, South Korea has developed and imported many new spiritual beliefs, values, and practices, giving South Koreans a wide variety of approaches to spirituality and creating fertile ground for the study of Korean spirituality. In North Korea, on the other hand, because of the tight control the North Korean government maintains over the lives of its citizens, expressions of spirituality are limited to a much narrower range, making the north a less appealing place for the study of spirituality. Nevertheless, a book that announces itself as a study of Korean spirituality cannot totally ignore developments in the People's Democratic Republic of Korea (North Korea).

One reason North Korean spirituality cannot be ignored is that there are active religious organizations in North Korea today. North Korea proclaims in its constitution that its citizens enjoy freedom of belief. It even allows the existence of official organizations for Buddhists, Protestant Christians, Roman Catholics, and followers of Ch'ŏndogyo. However, those organizations—the Chondoist Association, the Korean Buddhist Federation, the Korean Christian Federation, and the Korean Catholic Association—are under close government supervision. They are not allowed to proselytize and attract new members, and they are not permitted to operate many worship halls. There is only one Roman Catholic church in all of North Korea.

(At the time of this writing, in 2007, that church did not even have a resident priest.) There are also two Protestant churches, both in the capital of Pyongyang, though there are reports of some five hundred or so house churches scattered around the country. Buddhists fare somewhat better. There are currently sixty Buddhist temples open and operating, though they are maintained more as cultural treasures, reminding visitors of Korea's Buddhist heritage, than as actual sites for meditation, worship, or prayer. Ch'ŏndogyo is the most favored religion in North Korea. Because of its indigenous roots and its role in the Tonghak peasant rebellion in the 1890s—a rebellion North Korean historians define as a revolutionary anti-imperialist uprising—it is even permitted a token role in the North Korean government. The Ch'ŏndogyo Young Friends Party holds a few symbolic seats in the powerless North Korean parliament, the Supreme People's Assembly. (The Social Democratic Party provides similar representation for Christians, but is not for religious believers alone. It also represents intellectuals and former members of the bourgeoisie who are not Christian.) Ch'ŏndogyo, with fifteen thousand members, claims to be the largest religious organization in North Korea. However, it has only one large building set aside for its exclusive use for religious services. Believers who are unable to travel to Pyongyang gather for worship in some eight hundred small meeting halls in various cities and towns around the country.

The members of these small, state-controlled religious organizations, numbering fewer than fifty thousand in all, do not represent the mainstream of North Korean spirituality. The dominant form of spirituality in North Korea is not what would normally be called a religion, but instead is grounded in a political ideology that has grown to serve as the functional equivalent of a religion for most North Koreans. An ideology called "Juche" appeared in the 1960s as an assertion of national self-reliance. However, the term "Juche" has now been expanded to mean much more than economic and political autonomy for the nation of Korea; it now also means autonomy for the human race. Juche doctrine proclaims that human beings should break free of any dependency on God or other supernatural beings and realize that men and women, working together, can achieve all of their goals without any supernatural assistance.

Despite its rejection of theism and its political origins, there are several reasons for labeling Juche ideology a form of spirituality. First, it offers a solution to a problem all human beings face in their existence as separate and distinct individuals. It promises believers that, through membership in the Juche community, they can overcome death and gain immortality. According to Juche teachings, human beings exist only within societies. There is no human being who is totally alone, who has absolutely no relationships and no interactions with any other human beings. Human beings exist as social beings. This means that human beings will continue to exist even after their individual physical lives end, as long as the society that defined their existence continues to exist.

The Confucian roots of Juche thought are obvious. Confucians also defined human beings as social beings who existed only as members of a family and a society. However, Confucians argued that the only form of immortality available to individuals was being remembered by their descendants and disciples after their physical death. Juche offers a different way to overcome death. Juche says that because Juche will last until the end of time, all those who hold fast to Juche philosophy and unite within a Juche-based organization under the guidance of a leader who embodies Juche will enjoy an eternal sociopolitical life after their body has died. Because Juche defines human existence as communal existence, then as long as the community of which we are a member continues to exist, so will we.

With its promise of immortality through membership in the Juche community, Juche philosophy meets a defining criterion of spirituality: it promises practitioners that they can overcome the limitations of existence as isolated individuals. Juche functions as a form of spirituality in a number of other ways as well. For example, it offers an object of a spiritual gaze. That object is none other than Kim Il Sung, the first and forever president of North Korea.

Kim Il Sung first gained mythical status in the late 1930s when, as a young man, he led an armed band against the Japanese occupation of Korea and Manchuria. Though he did not single-handedly defeat the Japanese (despite North Korean claims to the contrary), he inflicted more damage on Japanese military and police forces than any other independence activist. Moreover, unlike most of his colleagues in the armed struggle against Japan, he was never captured. By 1945 he had become a symbol of Korean anti-Japanese nationalism and was given a hero's welcome when he returned after the Japanese defeat in World War II.

In 1948, when the United States and the Soviet Union divided Korea into two competing nations, Kim became the leader of the Communist government in the North and burnished his nationalist credentials by repeatedly calling for the two halves of Korea to unite. However, when a full-scale war to unify the two Koreas broke out in 1950 and ended in 1953 with Korea still divided, Kim convinced North Koreans that he had successfully resisted an American-led attack on the Korean nation. He also managed to adroitly maneuver Korea between China and the Soviet Union when the leaders of those two Communist countries had a falling out at the end of the 1950s. Kim first articulated Juche philosophy in the context of the Sino-Soviet split, insisting that Korea was a self-reliant country, dependent on neither the Soviet Union nor China.

As the leader of the North Korean government, Kim not only defended Korea's autonomy; he also provided food, housing, medical care, and employment for the North Korean population. Drawing on the traditional Korean view of the state as the personal possession of the ruling family, Kim presented his government's social welfare programs as personal gifts to the people from their leader. North Koreans were told that the rest of the world envied them because only North Koreans were privileged to live under such a fatherly leader.

Kim Il Sung is portrayed in Juche writings as a father figure for the entire nation and as the closest a human being can come to being a god without being an actual supernatural entity. Because he is seen as having protected the Korean nation from both external adversaries and economic adversity, North Korean publications describe Kim as "the sun of the nation and mankind." His son and current leader, Kim Jung Il, basks in the glory of being the favored son of such a heroic figure. They are described as the first and second most intelligent human beings who have ever lived.

North Koreans are repeatedly told that both Kims have risen to the status of the true masters of the universe that Juche says all human beings can become but no others have managed to achieve. Kim

Il Sung died in 1994, but the North Korean Constitution states that he is still and will forever be the president of his country. Through a slogan inscribed on a 92-meter-high Tower of Immortality in Pyongyang as well as on signs throughout their country, North Koreans are reminded daily that "The Great Comrade Kim Il Sung will always be with us." Their government has also adopted the Christian practice of dating years from the birth year of the founder of their religion. In North Korea, the year is not 2008; instead, it is Juche 97, counted from 1912, the year Kim Il Sung was born, as year 1. Moreover, instead of celebrating Christmas on December 25, North Koreans celebrate the Sun's Day on April 15, the day Kim Il Sung was born. The period from February 16 (Kim Jong Il's birthday) through April 15 is called the Loyalty Festival Period, the most festive period of the year in North Korea. Public celebrations are held throughout the country on the first and last days of this period, and in between, students are asked to demonstrate their loyalty by hiking in groups to sacred sites such as Kim Il Sung's birthplace. North Koreans see such treks as pilgrimages to sacred sites.

Like many other forms of spirituality, Juche has its supernatural elements. When Kim Il Sung died, birds were seen to weep. North Koreans are also told that on the night Kim Jong Il was born, three stars suddenly appeared in the sky above his purported birthplace. In subsequent years, his birthdays have been marked by such unnatural events as the appearance of double rainbows above that exact site, a log cabin on Korea's highest and most sacred mountain, Mount Paekdu. That log cabin has joined Kim Il Sung's birthplace in Pyongyang as a holy site visited by pilgrims and newlyweds.

According to the mass media in North Korea, though Kim Il Sung remains the brightest sun in the universe, his son Jong Il, as the living embodiment of his father's Juche philosophy, is the only savior active in the world at this time. Therefore, North Koreans, and all humanity, are urged to unite in ironclad unity around Kim Jong Il's leadership. Only by doing so can they create the eternal sociopolitical community that will build a paradise on this earth.

Most forms of spirituality provide guidelines for appropriate human behavior, and Juche philosophy is no exception. North Koreans are told that loyalty, reverence, and obedience are virtues all true

Juche believers should cultivate. Those are traditional Confucian virtues, but the focus of those virtues in Juche is much narrower than it was in Confucian Korea. North Koreans are told they should always be loyal to their current leader, display reverence for him and his father, and obey every word uttered by either of them. (There is no room in Juche Korea for the right of remonstrance that allowed Confucian scholars in premodern Korea to send written protests of government policies to their leaders.) North Koreans are also told they should always feel grateful for all the two Kims have done for them, from preserving their national independence in the anti-Japanese and anti-American wars of liberation to creating the workers' paradise that is North Korea today.

Such devotion to the leader and the Juche philosophy he embodies is often expressed through rituals that are like no rituals Korean Confucians have ever engaged in. For example, on special occasions North Koreans visit the 20-meter-high bronze statue of Kim Il Sung in front of the Museum of the Revolution in Pyongyang, bow before it, and lay flowers at its base. Foreign visitors to Pyongyang are expected to do the same soon after they arrive. When a North Korean couple marries, they both swear their loyalty to Kim Il Sung and Kim Jong Il and then visit a nearby statue of Kim Il Sung (there are said to be more than thirty-five thousand such statues in North Korea) and place flowers in front of it. They will then have their wedding picture taken with that statue in the background. In a final ritual display of belief in and reverence for the Juche philosophy, at a funeral mourners are supposed to cry out, "Though this body is deceased, the spirit of the revolution still lives."

Juche philosophy is not a religion per se, because Kim Il Sung is not worshipped as a god; he is respected as an exceptionally wise, benevolent, and talented human being. Nevertheless, because all other forms of spirituality are severely restricted in North Korea, Juche philosophy is the only form of spirituality available to the vast majority of North Koreans, who thirst for spirituality as much as citizens of other countries do. Juche followers believe in the tenets of Juche with the same religious fervor that followers of religions believe in their religion's tenets. Juche believers expect that their faith will be rewarded with immortality, as religious believers do. And Juche believers perform rituals that allow them to display respect for Kim Il Sung with the same solemnity shown by the devoutly religious when they worship their gods. In short, Juche philosophy has many religious overtones and at the very least qualifies as a form of spirituality. Therefore, no discussion of Korean spirituality would be complete without at least a brief discussion of the Juche ideology of North Korea.

Further Reading

This book provides a general overview of Korean spirituality. For more detailed information, the reader will need to do some additional reading, suggestions for which are to be found below. No attempt is made to provide a comprehensive list. Instead, I have tried to list material that is both reliable and readily available either in academic libraries or in bookstores.

For a survey of Korean religious history, see James Grayson, *Korea, a Religious History—Revised Edition* (Routledge Curzon, 2002). Grayson provides an overview of the history of religions in Korea from the earliest times to the present day. For a survey of what Koreans say and do when they are religious, see the translated documents in Robert E. Buswell, Jr., ed., *Korean Religions in Practice* (Princeton University Press, 2006). If you want a closer look at specific aspects of Korean spirituality, see Laurel Kendall and Griffin Dix, eds., *Religion and Ritual in Korean Society* (University of California, Berkeley Institute of East Asian Studies, 1987), which contains articles by several of the top scholars of Korean religion on topics such as Neo-Confucianism and shamanism. Also useful are the articles on Korean spirituality, including Buddhism and Christianity, in Lewis R. Lancaster and Richard Payne, eds., *Religion and Society in Contemporary Korea* (University of California, Berkeley Institute of East Asian Studies, 1997). JaHyun Kim Haboush and Martina Deuchler, eds., *Culture and the State in Late Chosŏn Korea* (Harvard University Asia Center, 1999) is a good book to turn to if you want to know more about Confucianism, shamanism, Buddhism, and Catholicism between 1600 and 1900.

Korean shamanism has been the subject of a number of scholarly works in English. Among the best of them are Keith Howard, ed., *Korean Shamanism: Revivals, Survivals, and Change* (Royal Asiatic Society, Korea Branch, 1998); Laurel Kendall, *Shamans, Housewives, and Other Restless Spirits* (University of Hawai'i Press, 1985); Boudewijn Walraven, *Songs of the Shaman: The Ritual Chants of the Ko-*

rean Mudang (Kegan Paul International, 1994); and Laurel Kendall, *The Life and Hard Times of a Korean Shaman: Of Tales and the Telling of Tales* (University of Hawai'i Press, 1988). Korean Buddhism is also the subject of scholarly analysis in English. Among the best studies in English are two books by Robert E. Buswell, Jr.: *The Zen Monastic Experience* (Princeton University Press, 1992) and *Tracing Back the Radiance: Chinul's Korean Way of Zen* (University of Hawai'i Press, 1991). The Korean Buddhist Research Institute at Korea's leading Buddhist university has provided English-language surveys of Korean Buddhist history in *The History and Culture of Buddhism in Korea* (Dongguk University Press, 1993) and *Buddhist Thought in Korea* (Dongguk University Press, 1994).

The best introductions to Confucianism in Korea are Michael Kalton, *To Become a Sage: The Ten Diagrams on Sage Learning by Yi T'oegye* (Columbia University Press, 1988) (also available at http://faculty .washington.edu/mkalton/); Roger L. Janelli and Dawnhee Yim Janelli, *Ancestor Worship and Korean Society* (Stanford University Press, 1982); and Keum Jang-tae, *Confucianism and Korean Thoughts* (Jimoondang Publishing Co., 2000).

Christianity in Korea has been the subject of a large number of scholarly studies. Among the best introductions are Robert E. Buswell, Jr., and Timothy S. Lee, *Christianity in Korea* (University of Hawai'i Press, 2006); Donald N. Clark, *Christianity in Modern Korea* (The Asian Society, 1986); and Chung-Shin Park, *Protestantism and Politics in Korea* (University of Washington Press, 2003).

There is less available on Korea's new religions than there is on the older traditions. Nevertheless, there are some books worth reading. Among them are Kwangsoo Park, *The Won Buddhism (Wŏnbulgyo) of Sot'aesan: A Twentieth-Century Religious Movement in Korea* (International Scholars Publications, 1997); George D. Chryssides, *The Advent of Sun Myung Moon: The Origins, Beliefs, and Practices of the Unification Church* (Macmillan, 1991); and Yong Choon Kim, *The Ch'ondogyo Concept of Man: An Essence of Korean Thought* (Pan Korea Book Corporation, 1989).

Korea is one of the most internet-savvy nations in the world. It is not surprising, therefore, that Korean spirituality has a Web presence in English. An informative paper on shamanism by Korean-American writer Heinz Insu Fenkl can be found at http://www.geocities.com/area51/rampart/2627/knives.html. For a short overview of the history of Buddhism in Korea, go to http://www.hm.tyg.jp/~acmuller/kor-bud/korbud-overview.html. For more on Korean Buddhism, go to http://bud.buddhapia.com/eng/. For information on the history of Roman Catholicism in Korea, go to http://www.cbck.or.kr/. That page will come up in Korean, but you can click on "English" in the upper right corner for an English history of Catholicism in Korea.

For a succinct history of Protestant Christianity in Korea, go to the *Korea Journal* on the Web, at http://www.ekoreajournal.net. In the archives for Summer 1995, you will find Andrew E. Kim, "A History of Christianity in Korea: From Its Troubled Beginning to Its Contemporary Success."

Many of Korea's new religions have a Web presence. For information on the Unification Church, go to http://www.unification.org/ or http://www.ffwpui.org/ (the Family Federation for World Peace and Unification). For information on Ch'ŏndogyo in English, go to http://www.chondogyo.or.kr/new/celist.htm. Information on Daesun Jinrihoe can be found at http://www.dsjr.org/. Information on Jeungsando is at http://www.jeungsando.org/. Information on Maum meditation can be found at http://eng.maum.org/. Information on Dahn World is available at http://www.dahnyoga.com/.

Index

ritual (continued):
initiation, 81, 143; Juche, 150; participatory, 72, 134–135; playful, 1;
Protestant, 72, 73; repentance,
143; ritual-based communities,
60; shamanic, 22–23, 102–104,
132–133; somber, 1; Tonghak, 81;
village, 139–140; worship, 122
Romance of the Three Kingdoms,
104
rosary: Catholic, 132; Ch'ŏndogyo,
131

sacraments, 66, 143
sacred texts, 143; Bible, 59, 61, 70,
74, 76, 136, 143; Ch'ŏndogyo, 117;
Confucian Classics, 30, 49, 52,
61, 70, 113; Daesun Jinri-hoe, 119;
Daoist, 70; new religions, 137, 143;
sutras, 30, 34, 41, 47, 61, 70, 130,
143; Tonghak, 81, 83; Unification
Church, 92, 137; Won Buddhist,
129
sacred trees, 31, 99, 103
sages, 14–17, 32, 67; becoming a
sage, 65–66; in Confucianism, 31,
48–49; as deity, 18, 101
saint, 16, 67–68
salvation, pursuit of, 69, 76, 122;
in Buddhism, 110; and Catholic
sacraments, 66; in Protestant
Christianity, 135; rites pertinent
to, 143; in the Unification Church,
92
samsin. See gods, goddess of fertility
and childbirth
sanggŭk, 88
sangsaeng (mutual overcoming), 88
Sanskrit, 72
Sedona, Arizona, 91
Seoul, 1, 39, 70, 76, 127, 139, 143

Seoul National University, 136
self-cultivation, 5, 6, 30, 46, 97,
112–113, 125, 144
selfishness, 9, 15, 17, 18, 26, 65, 85,
128, 131
sermon: Ch'ŏndogyo, 83; Christian,
136; new religions, 137; Taejonggyo, 137; Won Buddhist, 129
shamans, 14, 53; and ancestors,
26, 99; and Buddhism, 18;
charismatic, 20–23, 73; clients
of, 4, 6; dance, 140; and Daoism,
18; definition of, 20, 31–32;
divining, 21, 133; and ghost
weddings, 140; government
restrictions on, 63; healing, 24;
hereditary, 21–23; and hungry
ghosts, 27, 104; and initiation
rituals, 31–32; and lucky charms,
25; number of, 77; number of
followers, 4; offices of, 1; official
rituals, 24; ordinary rituals,
22–23, 102–104, 132–133; as ritual
specialists, 20; shrines of, 3; and
village festivals, 25, 139–140; and
women, 20–21, 25. See also spirit
possession, in shamanism; spirits,
and shamans
Shinto: and colonial rule, 63;
number of adherents, 4
Silla, 33, 55
sin, 62, 74, 92; absence of in folk
religion, 28–29; confession of, 143;
definition of, 28
sincerity, 49, 52, 53, 81, 83–84, 87–88,
94, 113
sinsŏn. See immortals
Social Democratic Party, 146
Soka Gakkai, 93
Sŏn, 36
Son Pyŏnghŭi, 117

About the Author

Don Baker teaches Korean civilization in the Department of Asian Studies at the University of British Columbia in Vancouver. He received his Ph.D. in Korean history from the University of Washington in 1983, with a dissertation on the Confucian confrontation with Catholicism in eighteenth-century Korea. He is a coeditor of *Sourcebook of Korean Civilization* from Columbia University Press (1996) and the author of *Chosŏn hugi yugyo wa ch'ŏnjugyo ŭi taerip* (The Confucian Confrontation with Catholicism in the Latter Half of the Chosŏn Dynasty), published by Iljogak in Seoul in 1997. He has also published numerous articles on Korean history, philosophy, religion, and traditional science. His current research focuses on the beliefs and values of the Confucian philosopher Chŏng Yagyong and on how the battles for religious freedom waged by Christianity, Ch'ŏndogyo, and other new religions have influenced the establishment of democracy in South Korea.

Production Notes for Baker / KOREAN SPIRITUALITY

Interior design by Rich Hendel, in 10-point Minion Pro,

with display type in Tarzana Wide.

Composition by BW&A Books, Inc.

Printing and binding by the Maple-Vail Book Manufacturing Group

Printed on 60# Text White Opaque, 426 ppi